Patrick H. Joyce ❖ Connie Mack ❖ Father William F. Davitt ❖ Sergeant Major Daniel Joseph Daly
ather Luis Batis Sainz ❖ Father José María Robles Hurtado ❖ Father Mateo Correa Megallanes
❖ Father Michael J. Ahern ❖ Alfred E. Smith ❖ John Edward Reagan ❖ Edralin
❖ Jorge J. Hyatt ❖ John Fitzgerald Kennedy ❖ Vincent T. Lombardi ❖ Major General Brady
W. McDevitt ❖ Harry E. McKillop ❖ Ronald A. Guidry ❖ Hilario G. Davide ❖ Alfred F. "Bud" Jetty
nt ❖ Father Thomas A. Mulcrone ❖ Paul E. Nollette ❖ Beryl D. Jones ❖ Steve Lopez ❖ John Whytal
eutenant Daniel O'Callaghan ❖ Captain Alfredo N. Fuentes ❖ Vincent P. Valerio ❖ Paul Marretti
d Letourneau ❖ James T. Mullen ❖ James B. Connolly ❖ William C. Prout ❖ Edward F. McSweeney
ph Daly ❖ Joyce Kilmer ❖ Dr. Claude Brown ❖ Father John B. DeValles ❖ George Herman "Babe" Ruth
er Miguel de la Mora ❖ Father Rodrigo Aguilar Alemán ❖ Father Pedro de Jesús Maldonado Lucero
George Willmann ❖ Myles E. Connolly ❖ Oscar Ledesma ❖ Ernest I. King ❖ Father William P. Ryan
. Rodríguez ❖ John W. McCormack ❖ Father Charles J. Watters ❖ Joseph A. Sullivan ❖ John W. McDevitt
Gannon ❖ Chris Godfrey ❖ Paul D. Scully-Power ❖ Robert Sargent Shriver ❖ Virgil C. Dechant
Judge William F. Downes ❖ Donald D. Lederhos ❖ Raymond L. Flynn ❖ Father Ronald P. Pytel
resti ❖ Daniel D. Sieve ❖ David P. Hessling ❖ Robert D. Wolf ❖ Ted van der Zalm ❖ Normand Letourneau

Patrick H. Joyce ❖ Connie Mack ❖ Father William F. Davitt ❖ Sergeant Major Daniel Joseph Daly
ather Luis Batis Sainz ❖ Father José María Robles Hurtado ❖ Father Mateo Correa Megallanes
❖ Father Michael J. Ahern ❖ Alfred E. Smith ❖ John Edward Reagan ❖ Father Isaias X. Edralin
❖ Jorge J. Hyatt ❖ John Fitzgerald Kennedy ❖ Vincent T. Lombardi ❖ Major General Patrick H. Brady
W. McDevitt ❖ Harry E. McKillop ❖ Ronald A. Guidry ❖ Hilario G. Davide ❖ Alfred F. "Bud" Jetty
nt ❖ Father Thomas A. Mulcrone ❖ Paul E. Nollette ❖ Beryl D. Jones ❖ Steve Lopez ❖ John Whytal
eutenant Daniel O'Callaghan ❖ Captain Alfredo N. Fuentes ❖ Vincent P. Valerio ❖ Paul Marretti
d Letourneau ❖ James T. Mullen ❖ James B. Connolly ❖ William C. Prout ❖ Edward F. McSweeney
ph Daly ❖ Joyce Kilmer ❖ Dr. Claude Brown ❖ Father John B. DeValles ❖ George Herman "Babe" Ruth
er Miguel de la Mora ❖ Father Rodrigo Aguilar Alemán ❖ Father Pedro de Jesús Maldonado Lucero
George Willmann ❖ Myles E. Connolly ❖ Oscar Ledesma ❖ Ernest I. King ❖ Father William P. Ryan
. Rodríguez ❖ John W. McCormack ❖ Father Charles J. Watters ❖ Joseph A. Sullivan ❖ John W. McDevitt
Gannon ❖ Chris Godfrey ❖ Paul D. Scully-Power ❖ Robert Sargent Shriver ❖ Virgil C. Dechant
Judge William F. Downes ❖ Donald D. Lederhos ❖ Raymond L. Flynn ❖ Father Ronald P. Pytel
resti ❖ Daniel D. Sieve ❖ David P. Hessling ❖ Robert D. Wolf ❖ Ted van der Zalm ❖ Normand Letourneau

BY THEIR WORKS

BY THEIR WORKS

PROFILES OF MEN OF FAITH WHO MADE A DIFFERENCE

Stephen Singular

Introduction by Carl A. Anderson

Produced by The Philip Lief Group, Inc.

Collins

An Imprint of HarperCollins*Publishers*

For information write: The Knights of Columbus Supreme Council,
One Columbus Plaza, New Haven, Connecticut, 06510.

Produced by The Philip Lief Group, Inc.
130 Wall Street, Princeton, New Jersey 08540

A list of photograph credits appears on page 140.

HarperCollins books may be purchased for educational, business,
or sales promotional use. For information please write:
Special Markets Department, HarperCollinsPublishers
10 E. 53rd Street, New York, NY 10022.

ISBN-10: 0-06-116145-4
ISBN-13: 978-0-06-116145-2

Printed in Korea

First Edition January 2006
10 9 8 7 6 5 4 3 2 1

ACKNOWLEDGMENTS

As all writers know, a work of this magnitude could only be accomplished with the invaluable contributions of a great many talented people.

First and foremost, for his initial vision of the work and by way of honoring the more than one million, seven hundred thousand devoted Knights of Columbus members, I want to extend personal thanks to Carl A. Anderson, Supreme Knight.

Also at the Knights' central offices in New Haven, Connecticut: Sue Brosnan, Mary Lou Cummings, Paul McGlinchey, Charles Lindberg, John Cummings, Tim Hickey, Ron Tracz, Kaitlyn McCarthy, Paul Devin, Andrew Walther, and Patrick Korten.

And to Fiorello B. Balitaan, Vice President and Assistant Corporate Secretary, Knights of Columbus Philippines.

The complicated and creative task of compiling and selecting images for this book fell to the folks in New Haven and, most significantly, to the talented team of professionals at The Philip Lief Group, in Princeton, New Jersey. At PLG, I want to thank the following: Philip Lief, Albry Montalbano, Judy Capodanno, and Annie Jeon. PLG invited their independent colleague, Donna Halper, into the project. Enough good cannot be said of Donna's writing, researching, and editing talents.

Thanks are also due to the families of many of the men profiled, who were generous with their time and who provided many family photographs for inclusion in this book.

CONTENTS

BY THEIR WORKS

Call him not heretic whose works attest

His faith in goodness by no creed confessed.

Whatever in love's name is truly done

To free the bound and lift the fallen one

Is done to Christ. Whose in deed and word

Is not against Him labours for our Lord.

When he, who, sad and weary, longing sore

For love's sweet service sought the sisters' door

One saw the heavenly, one the human guest

But who shall say which loved the master best?

John Greenleaf Whittier

INTRODUCTION

From the very first moment that the first Europeans set foot in the New World, the history of the Americas has been in many ways a history of religious faith.

Christopher ("Christ bearer") Columbus named the first island on which he landed San Salvador, for the savior, Jesus Christ. When his flagship, the Santa Maria (St. Mary), was wrecked on Christmas Day in 1492, he "took possession of a large town which I named the city of Navidad (Nativity)." Upon his return to Spain, he gave thanks to the "Eternal God our Lord who gives to all those who walk His way," and expressed enthusiasm at the prospect of "the conversion of so many peoples to our holy faith."

A little less than four hundred years later, Columbus' beloved Catholic Church had prospered in Canada and Latin America, but Catholics were a beleaguered minority in what was now the United States of America, mostly recent immigrants who were often the target of angry prejudice

"The First Landing of Columbus in the New World." Published by Charles deSilver, 1856–57.

The mall in Washington, D.C., is home to some of the world's finest museums, and affords views of, and opportunities to visit, many sites of American government and history.

But while it is easy to appreciate the significance of such priceless items as the Declaration of Independence and the original handwritten copy of the United States Constitution, few of the 16 million annual visitors to the mall know the significance of one aspect of the most imposing of the mall's landmarks, the Washington Monument. Part way up this 555-foot-tall obelisk, at the 152-foot level, the white marble stones undergo an unmistakable change in hue. Tour guides will usually explain that it's because construction was suspended for several decades when they ran out of money in the middle of the project. That's true, as far as it goes. But there's quite a bit more to the story.

Early in 1854, Pope Pius IX sent a gift to the people of the United States: a stone taken from the 2000-year-old Temple of Concord in Rome, for inclusion in the construction of the monument to the nation's first president. But it was a measure of the times that the reaction on the part of many Americans was not gratitude, but fear.

Catholics, who had been little more than a rare curiosity at the dawn of the American republic (there were only 30,000 Catholics in the entire United States when the Constitution was ratified, nearly all of them in Maryland), were by 1850 the largest single religious group in the country. And the rapid growth in their numbers generated an angry, sometimes violent backlash.

During the winter of 1853-54, rumors began to spread that placement of the Pope's stone in the monument was part of a ghastly plot; that the monument's completion would be a signal for a papal coup, delivering America into the hands of the man that many had come to regard as the "whore of Babylon." And so, in the middle of the night of March 6, 1854, a group of men stole the Roman stone, smashed it, and threw the rubble into the Potomac River. So much for the papist plot!

The men who ran off with the stone were members of the "Know-Nothings," a secret society of nativist anti-Catholic bigots that briefly became a powerful political party. In 1854 and 1855, the Know-Nothings made a dramatic showing in elections all across the country, electing the mayor of Philadelphia and more than a hundred members of the U.S. Congress. They were especially popular in New England: in Massachusetts they captured the governorship, every seat in the Massachusetts senate, and all but two seats in the state assembly. They rolled up majorities in Rhode Island, Connecticut, and New York, as well as in states in other parts of the country, including far-off California. Their platform included such proposals as barring Catholics from holding public office, on grounds that they owed allegiance to a "foreign prince" (the pope).

In the nation's capital, in the wake of the stone-smashing incident, Know-Nothings took over the Monument Society, a private organization that was building the Washington Monument with money appropriated by Congress. Soon, government funding was cut off and construction came to a halt. More than two decades would pass before work resumed.

This was the world into which Michael J. McGivney was born. He was a year and a half old at the time of the Washington Monument incident, the first child of Patrick and Mary McGivney, both natives of Ireland who had fled the potato famine to start a new life in America. His life was typical of Catholics in the United States at the time, where poverty and childhood disease made survival a constant struggle. There would be 12 more children in the McGivney family, only seven of whom would live to adulthood.

Father Michael J. McGivney.

Sunday morning Mass at the camp of the Fighting 69th in New York.

The years in which young Michael McGivney attended school were a wrenching, tumultuous time. As suddenly as their spectacular rise to power had come, the Know-Nothings collapsed as divisions over slavery tore the party apart, and the slavery issue replaced nativism and anti-Catholicism as the principal cleavage dividing American society.

Soon the entire nation was caught up in civil war, and that great cataclysm and its almost unimaginable slaughter changed American society forever. Michael was nine years old when the war began, and a few weeks before he turned ten, an Irish Catholic regiment from New York would fight in the first great battle of the Civil War, the First Battle of Bull Run. The Fighting 69th

would go on to become one of the most highly regarded units of the war, playing a major role at Antietam and Gettysburg; they remained with General Grant's Army of the Potomac to the very end and were at Appomattox when Grant accepted Lee's surrender. Hundreds of thousands of other Catholic immigrants fought in the war on both sides, and their bravery was matched only by their disproportionately heavy losses. When the last shot had been fired, even Grant, who had been known for his anti-Catholic views (he had briefly been a member of the Know-Nothings before the war), would readily concede their right to a place in American society.

One month before the Civil War ended, on March 4, 1865, President Lincoln proceeded to define post-war America in his second inaugural address, one of the greatest speeches in the nation's history:

"With malice toward none; with charity for all; with firmness in the right, as God gives us to see the right, let us strive on to finish the work we are in; to bind up the nation's wounds; to care for him who shall have borne the battle, and for his widow, and his orphan—to do all which may achieve and cherish a just and lasting peace among ourselves, and with all nations."

The future, in other words, would be one of reconciliation and charity, not recrimination and hatred.

Michael McGivney was still in school as Lincoln's words echoed throughout an exhausted nation. And he was still attending classes when the awful word came from Washington on April 15 that Lincoln had been assassinated. Like all Americans, Michael was deeply affected by Lincoln's tragic death, and profoundly moved by Lincoln's call for charity toward all, binding up the nation's wounds, caring for the widow and orphan, and his hope for a lasting peace. He would carry those sentiments with him for the rest of his life.

Just weeks after Lincoln's assassination, Michael left school at the age of 13 to help the family survive financially, taking a job in the spoon-making department of a brass factory. A few years later he would resume his studies at a Catholic school in Québec, where he now devoted all his energy to mastering subjects that would prepare him for the seminary.

In 1876, the Civil War now a decade in the past and the Know-Nothings a distant bad memory, Congress finally voted an appropriation of $2 million to finish the Washington Monument. The following year, Michael J. McGivney was ordained a priest in Baltimore's historic Cathedral of the Assumption. He began his priestly ministry at St. Mary's Church in New Haven, Connecticut on Christmas Day, 1877.

As a Catholic priest, Father McGivney struggled with the many problems that plagued most Catholic communities in America. While the Know-Nothings were long gone, a residue of anti-Catholic sentiment remained. A fire had destroyed the original wooden St. Mary's, and when a new stone church replaced it in July 1879, the *New York Times* headline read, "How An Aristocratic Avenue Was Blemished By A Roman Church Edifice."

His parishioners were mostly poor Irish working-class people. Too often the men, who spent their lives doing hard physical labor, drank hard and died young, leaving wives and children with no means of support. Moreover, their involvement with the church rarely extended beyond Sunday Mass, if they were seen there at all.

Though the odds seemed long, Father McGivney resolved to turn things around. Fraternal benefit societies had become popular in recent years, but few if any were aimed at Catholics. McGivney decided that such an organization would offer both an opportunity to provide financial support for families who'd lost the breadwinner, and an avenue by which to draw Catholic men closer to the church.

In February 1882, Father McGivney brought together a small group of two dozen men in the basement of St. Mary's Church for an organizational meeting. After some discussion, they decided to establish an organization named after Columbus, the New World's first Catholic evangelist. The handful of men in that church basement would eventually grow to nearly 1.7 million members, and would one day be described by Pope John Paul II as "the strong right arm" of the Catholic Church.

Members of the new "Knights of Columbus" would lead the way to respectability and acceptance for Catholics in American society. But they did much more than that. Stressing foundational principles of charity, unity and fraternity, they built an organization that would ultimately donate more than $130 million annually to charity, and become the backbone of parish life, devoting more than 60 million hours a year in volunteer service to their local churches and a multitude of other charitable endeavors. A fourth principle, patriotism, was soon added, and Knights led the way in demonstrating to all that love of God and love of country are not only compatible, but for every faithful Catholic citizen, inseparable.

Thirty years after the Order's founding and 420 years after Columbus first set foot in America, the Knights of Columbus had developed enough clout to persuade Congress to fund the construction of a Columbus Memorial in Washington, D.C. President William Howard Taft personally addressed the June 8, 1912, dedication, and he was joined at the ceremony by most of his cabinet, several Supreme Court justices and many members of Congress. Immediately after Taft's speech, a parade passed the reviewing stand in front of Union Station, led by 2,500 soldiers and sailors, followed by an astounding 20,000 Fourth Degree Knights in full regalia. The Order lobbied state legislatures to make Columbus Day a holiday (the first to do so was Colorado, in 1907), and in 1937 President Roosevelt proclaimed October 12 Columbus Day throughout the United States.

By design, Father McGivney shaped the Knights as an organization of Catholic laymen, and he declined to take a leadership role in the Order himself. His goal was to create a group in which men of faith would gather together and put their faith into action. They would do so with the encouragement of the church, but as members of an organization that was their own.

In just a few short years, Knights had put down roots in every state in the Union and in Canada,

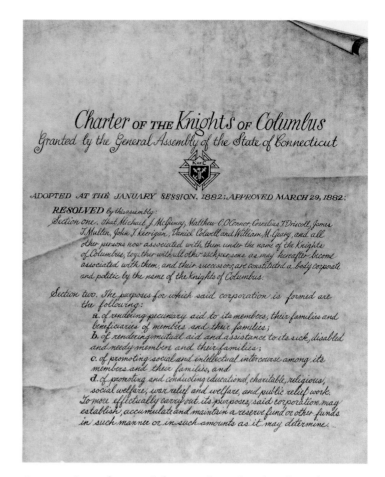

An artist's rendition of the Knights of Columbus charter approved on March 29, 1882.

Mexico, and the Philippines as well. When a brutal anti-clerical regime in Mexico engaged in a vicious persecution of the Catholic Church in the 1920s and '30s, Knights of Columbus were instrumental in getting the U.S. government to pressure the Mexican government to halt the beatings and murders of Catholics who refused to renounce their faith. Five Mexican Knights who were martyred during that dark period have since become saints of the Catholic Church.

During a resurgence of Ku Klux Klan activity in the United States in the 1920s, Knights of Columbus helped lead the battle against religious and racial intolerance. And when the Klan waged a successful campaign in Oregon to pass a law requiring all children to attend only public schools—thereby shutting down the entire Catholic parochial school system—the Knights of Columbus funded a legal challenge to the law all the way to the U.S. Supreme Court, where the case was won, preserving educational choice for all.

The first Catholic to run for president of the United States was a Knight. The first Catholic to win the presidency was a Knight. The first Catholic speaker of the U.S. House of Representatives was a Knight. The first man to win an Olympic medal in modern times was a Knight. The first major league baseball player to hit 60 home runs was a Knight.

The stories of all these famous men are all told in this book. But you'll also read the stories of ordinary not-so-well-known Knights who have done extraordinary things. And you'll discover that the vision Father McGivney had for the Knights of Columbus back in the late 19th century was exceptionally far-sighted. While other Catholic organizations have come and gone, we have prospered and grown significantly for more than a century. Long before the Second Vatican Council laid the groundwork for a greatly expanded role for the laity in the work of the Church, Father McGivney understood the value and extraordinary potential of a Catholic lay organization that was simultaneously dedicated to serving the church and its priests and bishops, and organizationally distinct, allowing it to offer leadership opportunities, fraternal friendship, and endless opportunities to do its work in creative and innovative ways.

Today, with the Second Vatican Council's teaching on "The Church in the Modern World" in hand, our work has shifted from the earlier struggle against prejudice and persecution to the contemporary responsibility for shaping the culture of the countries in which we live, and the quest for a peaceful world in which the basic human dignity of every person is respected and honored.

For all of the men profiled in this book, famous or not, religious faith was a formative part of their lives. And membership in the Knights of Columbus is a common thread that played a significant role in shaping their values, strengthening their faith, and inspiring their dedication to their fellow men. Moreover, for every Knight whose life is detailed in this book, there are tens of thousands more who are making a difference in their communities, their parishes, and their families. We would tell their stories, too, but we'd have to fill an entire library.

In a very real sense, the story of Catholics in North America and the Philippines over the past century has also been the story of the Knights of Columbus. It is an often amazing and inspiring story, a story of faith in action. And it is our privilege to present it to you here, as seen through the lives of Knights who are representative of the millions of men we have always been referred to proudly as "Catholic gentlemen."

Fourth Degree Knights at the annual Columbus Day ceremony at the statue of Christopher Columbus in front of Union Station on Capitol Hill in Washington D.C.

CHAPTER ONE

The Late 1800s & Early 1900s

James T. Mullen

A generation before the founding of the Knights of Columbus, during a terrible famine in Ireland, many families had left their homeland and sailed to the United States looking for a better life. They had found it, but they also found strong anti-immigrant and anti-Catholic hostility. All Irish-Americans, including Father McGivney, had felt the sting of that prejudice and seen its effects. He'd watched many young Catholic men drift away from the Church and join nondenominational secret societies, just to have a place to belong. He knew action was needed, so he decided to create an environment that would bring together men of similar backgrounds and give them a proud sense of being both American and Catholic. He also hoped to provide them with a broader social life that was connected to the Church. His vision soon became reality in the establishment of the Knights of Columbus.

Father McGivney was the guiding hand behind the new organization, but he worked with two contemporary fraternalists, Daniel Colwell and James T. Mullen, to develop the rituals. The early day-to-day running of the Order was left to Mullen, and he and Father McGivney defined the early Knights of Columbus and gave the group its distinctive character.

Mullen was born in New Haven in 1847 and in September 1861, at the age of 14, he enlisted and fought in the Civil War as a member of the 9th Infantry Regiment, Connecticut Volunteers. Because of illness, he was soon discharged. Following the war, he joined the Sarsfield Guards, a militia unit of Irish-American veterans that was part of the National Guard of Connecticut. Under Mullen's leadership, the Sarsfield Guards formed the Red Knights, a tightly knit Catholic fraternal society with a three-degree initiation rite, which offered member families a small death-benefit program. Mullen was the society's first Supreme Knight. In 1880, the Red Knights disbanded after a number of the men got married and didn't sustain their commitment to the organization, but Mullen had gained invaluable experience in conceiving and running this group. He'd discovered the value of regular meetings and rituals, and would soon apply what he'd learned to a new venture.

In February 1882, Father McGivney was holding gatherings at St. Mary's Church in New Haven and looking for someone to lead a new fraternal order. He believed that Christopher Columbus, a Catholic hero for many American immigrants, would be the perfect patron for this endeavor. Father McGivney saw Mullen as the natural choice to head the effort, and put him in charge of drawing up the articles of incorporation, which were filed on March 29 of that year. It was Mullen who wrote much of the Order's constitution and bylaws, and Mullen who gave the most guidance on the ceremonials; he wanted them to resemble the rites of passage on a man's journey to knighthood. It was Mullen who was credited with choosing the word "Knights"—as opposed to "Sons"—for the name. He also designed the new emblem, now recognized as the Order's symbol around the world.

Mullen became the first Supreme Knight and was present for the inaugural meeting of 19 of the original 38 councils in his home state and beyond its borders. He oversaw the Order's first parade in 1885 and helped launch the donation policy for widows, which would evolve into the organization's hugely successful life insurance program. His reign lasted only four years, but those critical days laid the foundation that launched the Knights as a legitimate fraternal society that would last and expand far beyond the dreams of its founders. Father McGivney had made a very astute choice for the new leader.

Sixty men came to the first meeting of the Order, held at St. Mary's in February 1882, and councils were soon cropping up throughout Connecticut. Irish-American men, just as Father McGivney had hoped, were finding a home away from home within these walls. By the mid-1880s, the Knights had, as Mullen put it when addressing the recent accomplishments of his fellow Knights, "passed the dangerous days of infancy" and reached the "splendid manhood on which our Order is made…I am not a prophet, nor yet the son of a prophet. There is a voice low and soft that tells me that many homes and many families in the future will bless your unselfish efforts—and that in years to come your names and deeds will be inscribed upon the rolls of modest honor."

In 1885, as Mullen prepared to step down as the first Supreme Knight, Father McGivney gave him a gold watch with a special inscription that signified his service to the young organization. That service has echoed during the following 120 years and into the 21st century. Every man who now enters the Order and passes through its ceremonial rites owes something to the imagination and efforts of James Mullen. He gave the Knights a tangible sense of promise when it was mostly an idea in the minds of a handful of men who wanted to make life more meaningful for themselves and others. He followed through on Father McGivney's vision and made it real, creating a place where Catholic men could share their experiences and their faith.

When Mullen died in July 1891, Judge D. J. Donohue eulogized him at St. Mary's. Gratitude colored every word the Judge spoke.

"Early and late," the Judge said, "in season and out of season, he gave freely, generously and lovingly his time, his money, and his labor…He was the eye, the hand, the foot and the very purse of the Order…With the saintly McGivney as the first Supreme Secretary and the noble Mullen as the first Supreme Knight, we can look back with just pride to the early days of the Order."

St. Mary's Church, New Haven, Connecticut, 1885.

Endowment paid by the Knights of Columbus to the wife of James T. Mullen upon his death.

James B. Connolly

The first Olympic Games were held in Greece nearly 2,500 years ago and continued until Emperor Theodosius stopped them in 393 A.D. For the next 1,500 years, they were dormant, although the idea of reviving them never entirely went away. Finally, in 1896, a French nobleman named Pierre de Coubertin brought them back to life in Athens. The United States had followed this development closely and decided to send a dozen young men to Greece to compete, but nobody gave them much of a chance. Europe was the center of the world, and its athletes were expected to dominate the Games. To qualify for the Olympics, all the young Americans had to do was fill out an entry form and pay their own way across the ocean. For many of them, going to Athens was more or less a lark, a chance to see the world and have some fun, but for 29-year-old James B. Connolly,

representing America in an international event was something he took seriously. He wasn't just representing his country, but also his neighborhood in South Boston and the Church that was the lifeblood of his community. The triple jumper wanted to win for the United States, but he also wanted to bring home the gold for Irish Americans and for the Catholicism that had nurtured him since birth. He was truly a young man on a mission.

James B. Connolly was born on October 28, 1868. His parents were poor Irish immigrants, and he was one of 12 children. He never went to high school, but instead, got a job working as a clerk in a Boston insurance company, before working with the Army Corps of Engineers. Although he had limited education at that time, he was eager to learn and was active in the Catholic Library Association. But athletics remained important to him. When he decided to compete in the Olympics in 1896, Connolly made the trip across the Atlantic on an 8,000-ton German steamer called the *Barbarossa*. When the ship docked in Naples, his wallet was stolen and the Italian police held him for so long that he was afraid of missing his train to Greece. After several hours, the police found his wallet; his money was gone but not his train ticket. Clutching the ticket and thanking the officers, he ran away from them at a full sprint and managed to catch his train just as it was pulling out of the station.

Before leaving the United States, Connolly and his teammates from the Suffolk Athletic Club had calculated that once they reached Athens, they would have 12 days to rest, get used to the climate, and practice for their events. That first night in Greece, after 16 straight days of travel, they decided to unwind at a party. Arriving back at their hotel rooms at 1 A.M., they spent an hour talking about the recent excitement. At 4 A.M., they were awakened by a marching band practicing right beneath their windows. It was too loud for anyone to sleep so they kept talking. At 9 A.M., while they were eating breakfast, an official Olympic delegation announced that the Games would begin at 2 P.M.—that afternoon. Because the local population used a different calendar, the Americans had miscalculated the start of the Olympics by a full 11 days. With almost no sleep, they made their way over to the stadium, where the Olympics officially commenced for the first time in more than 1,500 years.

Connolly's event—known as the "hop, skip, and jump"— followed the opening ceremony. His first effort wasn't particularly good because he was running into a stiff wind and the pathway for the jump was newly laid and still soft. He'd had trouble getting traction and was worried that this problem would defeat him. Just before making his next attempt, Connolly paused, held his hands up in front of him, and breathed on them slowly, feeling the air move across his fingers, gathering his strength and concentration. In that moment, something unusual passed through him— a "rush of energy," he later called it, "like a warm wave going through my blood." Some observers close to Connolly were certain that he was praying. When the rush of energy subsided, he coiled his muscles, took off down the runway, and leaped into the air, sailing farther than he ever had. He jumped a total of 45 feet and was in first place. No one would catch him that day or even come close. He'd out-jumped the other competitors by three feet.

After making his winning leap, the redhead from Boston broke his concentration long enough to look up at the beautiful marble stadium. For the first time, he noticed that 150,000 people were watching him. He realized that many were now standing and cheering for him, and then he picked out a group of sailors in the stands wearing blue jackets; he knew they were Americans who'd left their docked ship to see their countrymen compete. They were waving at him and yelling out his name: "Connolly! Connolly! Connolly!"

It hit him that he was the first Olympic champion in more than 1,500 years, and the first American Olympic gold medal winner ever.

The band that had been playing beneath his window a few hours earlier struck up the "Star-Spangled Banner" and people everywhere were shouting at him: "Nike! Nike!" It means "The winner! The winner!"

Connolly was silent, gazing at the entire scene and grasping that his Olympic dream had come true. He'd accomplished what he'd come for and made his fellow citizens and Catholics proud. He'd put America on the worldwide sporting map. In future decades, Connolly would go on to be a war correspondent for the *Boston Globe*, join Back Bay Council 331 of the Knights of Columbus in Boston, and write 25 novels and more than a hundred short stories about sea adventures. His writings appeared in popular magazines like *Saturday Evening Post* and *Colliers*. He even attempted, unsuccessfully, to run for political office. But till he died, on January 20, 1957, he never forgot that glorious day in Athens. James Connolly had done something not just for himself or his teammates but for everyone across the United States, as well as for his community and his faith. It was the start of a great American Olympic tradition.

Cover of a July 1932 issue of Columbia *magazine depicting James B. Connolly winning the "hop, skip, and jump" event at the 1896 Olympics.*

William C. Prout

Born in South Boston on December 24, 1886, and coming of age with a thin body and poor health, William Prout seemed destined to be physically weak and limited in his expectations. Yet this condition only made him more determined to overcome the odds and turn himself into a fighter for his beliefs and convictions. William Prout fought his entire life for his Catholic principles and what he felt the Knights of Columbus could achieve. Some members of the Order have contributed spectacular deeds on battlefields, or in politics, the arts, or athletics. They've made headlines and become widely known to the general public. But other Knights left a legacy that unfolded behind the scenes. They managed the details, expanded the vision and mission, corrected mistakes or potential mistakes, and got

things done. They set the tone and the standard for what it means to be an active Catholic and a Knight in service to one's community—and they encouraged others to live up to it. They have been the backbone, the starting point, for everything else.

Prout was that kind of leader—constantly setting an example for others to follow, and reminding the membership that it could always do more. He was quietly fearless, incorruptible, self-sufficient, a man who had no use for falsehood or deception. He was plain-spoken and wanted above all to move the organization forward so that it could serve others long after he was gone. Competitive sports were his passion, but building the Order was his lifelong goal. In 41 years, he gave everything he had to make it happen.

Prout graduated from Boston University with a law degree, and while studying, he kept his body in superb shape by training as a quarter-miler and as an anchorman on the relay team. He represented Brown University in the New England Intercollegiate Athletic championships, and in 1908 he represented the American team that competed in the London Olympics; he ran the 400 meters, and although he didn't win, he was invited to meet President Roosevelt, along with his other teammates. He became active in the Amateur Athletic Association, and at the 1916 convention in New York, he was elected Second Vice President. During World War I, Prout was put in charge of athletics at Camp Dodge, Kansas, where he kept the soldiers in excellent condition. By 1922, he was president of the Amateur Athletic Union, a position to which he was reelected several more times during the 1920s. He was also chosen to lead the American delegation at the Amsterdam Olympics in 1928. As he rose within amateur sports, he also became more and more prominent as a Knight. In 1914–15, he served as Grand Knight of Back Bay Council 331, and from 1915–18 as district deputy. For the next three years, he was state secretary and in 1921 he was elected Massachusetts State Deputy. Under his leadership, statewide membership in the Knights reached its peak.

The foundation for strengthening and growing the Order, he was certain, was the life insurance business, and he used his State Deputy's office to make this point. If individual Knights had a financial stake in the organization, they would be more committed to working for its improvement. Prout was also passionate about education, starting a fund drive in 1921 for several Boston College construction projects. Two years later, he led the state convention in condemning an Oregon school bill for violating the rights of parents to direct the education of their children. He fought for the right of Catholic parents to choose the schools they wanted for their kids. By 1923, the U.S. Supreme Court had come down on Prout's and the Order's side in this argument, declaring the Oregon law unconstitutional.

Prout was highly supportive of the efforts of Brother Edward F. McSweeney to publish books that revised and deepened the understanding of American history, especially the history of ethnic groups across the nation. At Prout's urging, the Order created a fund sponsoring history books written by notable Americans, such as George Cohen's history of American Jews and W. E.B. DuBois's history of American blacks. Prout offered the proposal that launched the Columbian Squires, and in 1922 he instituted the annual Knights of Columbus Track Meet in Boston, one of the most popular events of the day.

By the mid-1920s, his hectic schedule and longstanding health battles began to catch up with him. Despite his failing health, he continued to take on more and more work for the Order. In 1922, he had been elected a Supreme Director and by that time, his reputation inside the organization had spread far beyond Massachusetts. In 1924, he was granted a private audience with the Holy Father in the Vatican at Rome. Pope Pius XI named him a Knight of the Order of St. Gregory the Great, and after receiving this honor, Prout felt the need to accomplish even more. But on the afternoon of August 4, 1927, just as he was preparing to lead the American Olympic delegation, he suddenly died at his home in Boston, at the age of 40. The newspapers said he had been ill for several months. It wasn't until he was gone that the membership realized how many things Prout had been involved in, and how much he'd gotten done in his few years as their leader. Many of his ideas would drive the Order forward for decades after his death. That was no accident because he'd set it up precisely that way.

At his funeral, one of the observers said it best. "Willam Prout died because he gave too much."

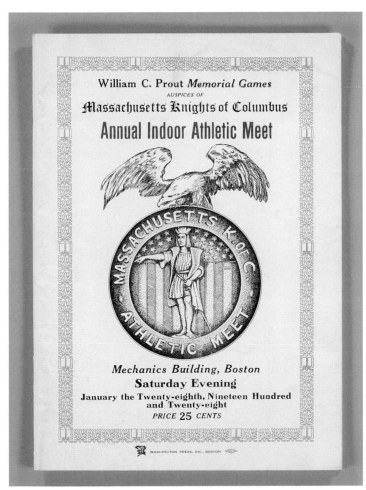

Cover of a program from the William C. Prout Memorial Games sponsored by the Massachusetts Knights of Columbus on January 28, 1928.

Edward F. McSweeney

What Edward F. McSweeney lacked in formal education he more than made up for with a passion for knowledge, a talent for leadership, an intense patriotism and a strong appreciation of the importance of history.

Edward McSweeney was the first of eight children born to John and Mary McSweeney in Marlboro, Massachusetts, while the Civil War still raged in 1864. He attended the Marlboro public schools, but as the oldest son, he was expected to start earning money as soon as possible, and so at thirteen he left school and began working as a shoemaker. He still continued to read voraciously, and his inquisitiveness, keen mind, and leadership qualities soon carried him well beyond the cobbler's trade.

He was among the founders of the Lasters' Union (a laster performed the difficult and specialized task of fastening a shoe's "upper" to the sole, using a "last," or mold, during the process). At age 21, he was editor of the new union's paper, and from 1886 until 1902, he served as general president of the union. Along the way, he served as the Massachusetts publicity organizer for President Grover Cleveland's reelection race in 1892, and the following year, he was appointed Assistant U.S. Commissioner of Immigration at Ellis Island, a post he held until 1902.

In February 1897, McSweeney became a member of the Knights of Columbus at Dongan Council 164 in New York. A few years later he transferred to Columbus Council 116 in Dorchester, Massachusetts. By 1905, McSweeney was back in the newspaper business, as editor-in-chief of the *Boston Traveler*, a position he would hold until 1910. He used his writing and lecturing skills—and his beliefs about human dignity and social justice, which were an outgrowth of his Catholic upbringing and background in the trade union movement—to promote improved health care and safer working conditions. McSweeney was chairman of the Boston Consumptives Hospital Trustees and was a key player in developing advanced treatment for tuberculosis patients. He campaigned for a state workman's compensation statute, and then helped administer the new law as a member of the Massachusetts Industrial Accident Board.

The period immediately following World War I was a turbulent time, when the anti-Catholic nativism and anti-immigrant fervor of the mid-1800s returned with a 20th-century flavor. A new surge of more than 400,000 European immigrants, especially from Catholic countries in southern and eastern Europe, flooded into the United States during the first 18 months after the armistice, and the Ku Klux Klan quickly seized on the fears generated by the new wave of immigration. An "Americanization" movement that had sprung up during the war (aimed especially at German immigrants) now evolved into a hostile and racist campaign aimed at all immigrants. It was accompanied by a trend among some historians to describe the history of America as purely Anglo-Saxon, with virtually no acknowledgment given to the contributions of non-English settlers in the New World. When these historians began to have a significant impact on the history textbooks, McSweeney rebelled.

He joined with the Supreme Master of the Fourth Degree, John H. Reddin (see page 10), in proposing a Knights of Columbus Historical Commission that would "investigate the facts of history as applicable to our country, to correct historical errors and omissions, to amplify and preserve our national history, to exalt and perpetuate American ideals, and to combat and counteract anti-American propaganda." The 1921 Knights of Columbus convention backed his vision, and McSweeney was named the commission's chairman.

Under McSweeney's leadership, the Knights of Columbus Historical Commission invited history professors, school teachers, students of American history and foreign relations, and others with an interest in the subject to submit manuscripts that would present original research in the field. Awards of up to $7,500 would go to the top winners. The result was a remarkable collection of papers that were both accessible and scholarly. Among the top award winners was history professor Samuel Flagg Bemis, who wrote *Jay's Treaty: A Study in Commerce and Diplomacy*. Bemis went on to become Sterling Professor of Diplomatic History at Yale, and won the Pulitzer Prize twice. Newspaper editor Allan Nevins, whose Knights-sponsored book *The American States During and After the Revolution, 1775–1789*, was his stepping-stone to academic life, ultimately became one of the most highly regarded historians of the 20th century. Other extraordinary monographs published by the Knights of Columbus thanks to McSweeney included *The Gift of Black Folk*, by the great African American scholar W.E.B. DuBois, and *The Jews in the Making of America* by George Cohen. McSweeney himself contributed a number of booklets to the series. The net result was a conclusive body of unassailable research and writing that demonstrated how America was the product of contributions by a remarkable array of people from all over the world. And McSweeney, who had his own interest in Irish history, and served as a vice president of the American Irish Historical Society, never tired of reminding everyone that all of the immigrant groups deserved proper credit for the part they'd played in making America great.

Driven by McSweeney's energy and intelligence, the Knights of Columbus filled significant holes in the popular understanding of U.S. history, bringing to readers the ideals of racial equality, and the principles of the Founding Fathers.

Once the Historical Commission had completed its work, he turned his energies toward the educational system in his home state. He built several schools in rural Massachusetts, where elementary and middle students could have access to the materials he'd either written or published, and he was making plans to construct even more schools.

In November 1928, as the 63-year-old McSweeney was launching a new effort to spread his educational message across New England, he died as a result of injuries he received during a car accident in Framingham, Massachusetts. But his legacy, in the form of the books he'd inspired and the ones he'd written, had an influence that lived on long afterward. Decades later, as the debate over civil rights began to widen and deepen in the United States, people would turn to writers such as W.E.B. DuBois to understand our entangled racial history. McSweeney's vision had helped make these resources possible.

He saw deeply into America's past and far into our future. History, his lifelong passion, would ultimately vindicate his conviction that the United States was the proud product of an almost infinite variety of people drawn to a common cause by a shared devotion to the principles of the American founders. Eventually, the country would be able to see just how far ahead of his time Edward McSweeney had been.

Three monographs published by the Knights of Columbus Historical Commission.

John H. Reddin

In much the same way that St. Paul was the early Church's apostle to the Gentiles, John H. Reddin was the Knights of Columbus's apostle to the American West and beyond. In the early years of the Order, Knights were to be found primarily in the East, which was to be expected for a group founded in Connecticut and limited by the transportation infrastructure of the day. But if the organization was to establish a truly national presence, pioneers were needed to carry the flag westward, and beyond American borders.

John H. Reddin was born in Seneca County, New York, in the town of Varick, on October 13, 1858. He was the son of Irish immigrants, and his father was involved in construction for the New York Central Railroad. John grew up in

Oneida and then Norwich, New York. He studied law and was admitted to the bar of the State of New York in 1880. That year, the young lawyer moved west with his father and family. Only four years earlier, Colorado had become a state and its mining resources were turning Denver into a boomtown. He settled in 1881 in what would one day be called the Mile High City, finding a community receptive to new ideas. He opened his own law practice there in April of that year, and for a time, served as assistant district attorney in Denver. He then went back into successful private practice as a lawyer. *The History of Colorado*, published during Reddin's lifetime, noted that "[h]is activities have always been of a helpful character, contributing to progress and improvement through intellectual development and moral uplift, and the consensus of public opinion places him in the front rank among Denver's representative men."

With the Order primarily an East Coast enterprise, the Knights hired "national organizers" to help spread the message to the newly developed areas of the United States. One such organizer was James J. Gorman of Fall River, Massachusetts, who met Reddin in Denver. In November 1900, Gorman and Reddin organized Denver Council 539, with Reddin heading the committee that chose the initial 58 applicants for charter membership, and then becoming the Council's first Grand Knight. After that fateful meeting with Gorman, Reddin soon proved that he was not just a great lawyer, but one of the most impressive organizers in the history of the Order. It wasn't long before Reddin was appointed Territorial Deputy of the Far West, and for 33 years, from 1907–1940, he was the Supreme Director of the Order for the western half of the United States, the longest record of service for anyone in that position. As Territorial Director, he launched Councils in El Paso, Texas; Butte, Montana; Salt Lake City, Utah; Portland, Oregon; Seattle; and San Francisco and Los Angeles, California. In the first decade of the 20th century, John Reddin was the key figure in spreading the Order across the American West and turning the Knights into a truly national organization. He traveled tens of thousands of miles by car to set up Councils from the Rockies to the Pacific Ocean, and in 1906 he journeyed outside the United States for the first time. In Mexico City, he helped found Guadalupe Council 1050. And he also played an important role in the order's growth in Canada's maritime provinces, making a trip there in 1911 to speak in St. John's, Newfoundland. As Reddin's efforts bore fruit, he was elected Colorado's first State Deputy.

As an innovator and authority on fraternal rites, he was selected chairman of the Ceremonial Committee, revising the First, Second, Third, and Fourth Degree rituals, but his innovations didn't stop there. He had a natural flair for promotion and spreading the word on what the Knights could do for a community or region. As Supreme Master of the Fourth Degree, he implemented a contest that offered cash prizes to students in secondary schools and academies for their essays on American government and history. Many of these students first learned about the Knights through these contests, and went on to become members of the Order. Reddin himself wrote that the essay contest was "the answer of the Knights of Columbus to all organizations which seek to batter down the Constitution, and to deprive any portion or class of our citizenship of their constitutional rights." He wanted everyone to know that the Knights of Columbus was a patriotic institution.

Reddin himself was also a historian and a talented and prolific writer. Thus—at a time when anti-Catholicism was very real, as Al Smith (see page 38) would find out seven years later—it was no surprise that in 1921, at the San Francisco Convention, Reddin helped establish the Knights of Columbus Historical Commission; it eventually published thirteen volumes on American history and related subjects. The idea behind the series was to include those contributions to the history of the United States by Catholics, Blacks, Jews, and others who were routinely neglected in history books. It was also Reddin who appointed Edward McSweeney (see page 8) as chairman of this project.

A frail man who never looked robust or enjoyed great physical health, Reddin was constantly active on behalf of the Order and a pioneer in every sense of the word. He demonstrated to everyone who met him or heard him speak the grand lesson that it isn't the flesh that determines one's strength or effect on life, but the force of one's spirit, mind, and heart.

In the 1920s, when the Ku Klux Klan was experiencing a surge of interest in Colorado, Reddin employed his legal skills to fight against the racists and protect Denver's minority citizens. Relentless in battling for equality and fairness, he was one of the most prominent attorneys in the West, but his reputation spread far beyond the Rocky Mountains— Pope Pius XI made him a Knight of St. Gregory. When he died in 1940, at age 82, the Order was established not only in the western United States but in other countries as well. The growth was just beginning and would exceed even Reddin's dreams.

The vision that he exemplified when first going West in 1880 took root throughout North America and the Philippines. Men like him had worked and traveled endlessly to turn the Knights into the world's largest Catholic family fraternal organization, which by 2005 had more than 12,000 councils and 1.7 million members around the globe. The same pioneering spirit that had built America from coast to coast had driven John Reddin to take his energy westward, and thanks to his tireless efforts, the Knights became a welcome home for Catholic men all over the United States.

Supreme Officers and Directors of the Knights of Columbus, Chicago 1932. Reddin is in the second row, fourth from the left.

Patrick H. Joyce

Rags-to-riches stories are about more than money and success. In the case of Patrick H. Joyce, the story is about a man who had to hit bottom before he could begin his extraordinary climb to the top. And it's also the story of the way his faith and ability to bounce back sustained him in good times and bad.

Born in Chicago, Joyce was raised during the 1880s in a colorful neighborhood known as the "Back of the Yards," on Chicago's South Side. Located just behind the thriving Union Stockyards, the area was loaded with character and characters. Almost every block hosted a tavern. All the families were struggling and much of the population was made up of Catholic immigrants whose social lives centered around the local parish. Two values dominated the "Back of the Yards": a belief in hard work and a bedrock attachment to the Catholic Church. Kids hawked newspapers on street corners, and horses clattered along the brick pavement on their daily milk runs. Houses were jammed together and the sharp smell in the air came from the slaughtering of livestock. It was a gritty part of town—the kind of place that ambitious young men hoped to leave behind, through education or other means.

Young Patrick attended Greene Elementary School, but was never much of a student. He had trouble sitting still in classrooms and gave up on education after only a couple of years. He was energetic and strong, throwing himself into the jobs available to a kid with his background in 1890s' America. He pushed a salt truck around a packing plant, was a switchman's apprentice on the Chicago & Alton Railroad, ran errands for a law office, labored in a hardware store, sorted iron in a junkyard, and apprenticed at a fertilizer plant. Eventually, the handsome young Irishman took a step up, making his way to the Chicago Board of Trade where he donned a linen suit and worked as a messenger. When he wasn't punching the clock, he liked to go to the racetrack with his Board of Trade friends and bet on horses. Sometimes he won and sometimes he didn't, but he managed to cash enough tickets to keep visiting the track. Then one day, he lost all of his savings gambling. It seemed like the worst thing he'd ever experienced, but it was just what he needed.

When he got home that evening, dead broke and depressed, his father was very upset with him and let Patrick know it. He was now in his twenties and the time had come, the older man made clear, for him to take care of himself— outside of their house. From now on, his bills and his debts were his own. With nothing in his pockets, Patrick took off and went down to the rail yard, jumping aboard a passenger train. An employee on the train knew him and asked him to lend a hand with unloading some goods at the next stop. He repeated this effort at the next stop and the one after that. He worked all night, until he was exhausted and filthy—his first real experience with railroading. The following night he did exactly the same thing. The railroad bosses told him they could use a hardworking hand like him, so for two years he stayed with the job, earning little more than food and a bed.

He loved the railroad but this line of work was going nowhere and he was very tired of sleeping in train cars. He quit for a job in a chain shop in East Chicago, Indiana, and when the shop owner decided to sell out, Joyce went into business for himself, peddling steel and iron. This brought him his first success and he soon opened a bolt shop in Chicago, which also did well.

In 1905, Joyce became a charter member and the first Grand Knight of Daniel Dowling Council 1063 in Chicago. Many years later, he said that the lessons taught in the Order's degree ceremonies had been a guide for him throughout the rest of his life.

When the bolt shop became bigger than the chain shop, he opened another business repairing railroad cars. He was back where he wanted to be—working in the rail industry—

but now he had a good income and a bed of his own. He began manufacturing railroad cars and by 1928 he was running three large plants. He was so busy that he could no longer devote as much time to the Knights as he wanted to.

"I had to drop out of active participation in a work I found most inspiring," he once said of the Order, "but I still prize my membership and look forward to the day when I can get back in the harness. In its field there is no better organization, and every young man eligible for membership should join. Its lessons are of permanent value."

With his earnings from the three manufacturing plants, Joyce bought stock in the Chicago Great Western Railroad. He bought more and more until he was the single largest shareholder. By November 1931, he had become company president. The man who'd ridden the rails like a hobo was now operating one of the nation's largest railroads. And the wealthier he became, the more he gave back to the community and the church. Joyce was grateful for all the opportunities he'd been given, even the opportunity to learn how to survive without a dime in his pocket or a place to rest his head; what he learned ultimately enabled him to prosper. And he was especially grateful to the Catholic church and the Knights of Columbus for teaching him the values that helped him succeed.

A Chicago Great Western Railroad train.

Connie Mack

In the long history of baseball, no major league team has ever been better—or worse—than the Philadelphia/ Kansas City/Oakland Athletics. Over the past hundred years, they've been up and down more than any other franchise, but their greatest days came under the leadership of a stiff-looking gentleman who came to the ballpark every day dressed in a suit, a tie, and a formal hat. Born on December 22, 1862, in East Brookfield, Massachusetts, he was baptized with the name of Cornelius Alexander McGillicuddy, but that handle didn't last long around the baseball diamond, where sooner or later almost everyone ends up with a nickname. By the time he reached adulthood, everybody called him Connie Mack.

Mack was the third of seven children in a large Irish Catholic immigrant family. At a young age he was active in the Church and also drawn to baseball. These two things— the moral foundation he was given through his religious training and his love of baseball— would shape his life and the future of the game. He was serious-minded, and this affected everything he did. He learned to play baseball while laboring in a shoe factory to help support his mother, a widow. He grew up as baseball itself matured and spread to cities and small towns across the country, and he was instrumental in building the summer game into America's national pastime.

Mack had played the sport with friends and classmates before becoming a professional catcher in the Connecticut State League. In 1884, he signed on with the Meriden (Connecticut) squad for $90 a month, and soon moved on to Hartford and then to Buffalo, where he became part owner of that team. Mack passionately believed in baseball's future and invested his life savings of $500 in the Buffalo nine. He lost every penny, which shaped his attitude about the relationship between pro sports and money for the rest of his career.

In 1901, he became the manager and owner of the dreadful Philadelphia A's of the upstart American League. The National League had been in existence since 1869, but the rival league was just making its debut and having trouble fielding competitive teams. The A's were so bad that the legendary New York Giants skipper John McGraw dubbed the team a "white elephant" that nobody in baseball would want to be associated with, let alone watch them play. Connie Mack took McGraw's remark as a personal challenge; he not only committed himself to making the Athletics win-ners, but put the image of an elephant on every uniform. A century later, the elephant has become the enduring symbol of the franchise and is still worn by the Oakland A's today. For the first half of that century, from 1901–1951, Mack ran the Philadelphia team from top to bottom like a no-nonsense executive would run a growing corporation.

He rarely raised his voice or scowled, but when he did, the players came to full attention. The Catholic values he'd absorbed as a youngster were demonstrated each day at the ballpark. He saw the dignity of every player and handled all of them fairly. He treated everybody the same, regardless of their statistics or salary. Mack commanded the respect of everyone who ever wore the A's uniform—and by commanding respect for himself, he commanded respect for baseball. The demeanor of this longtime Knight (Santa Maria Council 263 of Flourtown, Pennsylvania) gave the game continuity and purpose that reflected his values. His methods gave the A's a solid anchor and produced results on the field.

In 1901, the A's were truly awful, but by 1905 they were playing for the world championship and lost to McGraw's Giants. From 1910–14, the Athletics won four pennants and three World Series, exacting sweet revenge against McGraw by beating the Giants for the title in 1911 and '13. As a former catcher, Mack had a keen eye for pitching talent and over the years he signed some of the game's best arms: Rube Waddell, Jack Coombs, Chief Bender, and Eddie Plank. He also managed several of baseball's greatest hitters: Tris Speaker, Jimmie Foxx, and Ty Cobb. Connie Mack built two dynasties in Philadelphia, between 1910–14 and 1929–31, winning a total of nine pennants and five World Series. Along the way, he set records—for the most games managed, won, and lost—that may never be broken. He taught his players one lesson above all: because baseball doesn't run on a time clock like other team sports, the game is never over until the last man is out. Give everything you have, and don't ever quit.

Tall, thin, and dressed in customary dark suit and tie, he looked as if he meant business and ran his baseball affairs with absolute rectitude. It was a style that was built to last. His on-field and off-field leadership survived the early decades of the 20th century, when baseball was establishing itself on the American sporting scene. It survived the World Series gambling scandal of 1919, which threatened to discredit the game, it survived the hard times of the Great Depression and World War II; and it lasted into the 1950s, when baseball entered the modern era of tremen-

dous expansion, success, and media exposure. Mack was there every step, building the foundation and tradition that would make baseball America's most popular sport. But he never lost sight of what was most important. He was known for never missing Mass, and he did not like his players to use profanity. Mack was there to commend his brother Knight Babe Ruth (see page 30) to God at Ruth's funeral.

The game was his only source of income and since this was long before the days of radio or TV broadcasts, he could only generate money by selling tickets or peddling concessions. Win or lose, in good years and bad, Mack paid for the team's expenses from his own pocket. Twice he was forced to dismantle his lineup because he couldn't afford to pay all his stars. Many times, he thought about getting rid of the team or shutting it down when bankruptcy loomed, but he persevered and left his imprint on the early decades of the game. In 1937, he was named to the Baseball Hall of Fame in Cooperstown, New York. And in 1954, former colleagues and fans honored him there with a clay bust. It reads, "Mr. Baseball, you will live in our hearts forever."

A faithful Catholic to the end, the longtime Knight died shortly after receiving the last rites, on February 8, 1956, at the age of 93. Sports writer Red Smith wrote of him, "Connie entered the game when it was a game for roughnecks. He saw it become respectable, he lived to be a symbol of its integrity, and he enjoyed every minute of it."

This statue of Connie Mack, dedicated in 1957, stands outside Citizens Bank Park, home of the Philadelphia Phillies.

CHAPTER TWO

World War I

Father William F. Davitt

During World War I, the German army didn't observe a cease-fire for burial of the dead. The German troops stayed in their trenches and kept shooting round after round at the Allied soldiers lined up against them. This made the job of priests like Father William F. Davitt especially dangerous; Father Davitt was determined to give the fallen soldiers a proper memorial service even if bullets were flying. He was one of many courageous ordained Catholics who had gone to Europe to serve the American military in its first truly international conflict. During the fiercest battles, priests were often in the line of fire as they tried to perform their duties. And sadly, there would be times when it was one of these priests who needed a proper burial.

During World War I, the Knights of Columbus sponsored more than 50 chaplains who were sent to minister to Catholic soldiers. All these men were heroes for serving their faith and their country on the front lines, but among the most heroic was Father Davitt of Holyoke Council 90.

Born on January 6, 1886, in Holyoke, Massachusetts, and ordained in 1911 as a priest of the Springfield, Massachusetts, Diocese, Father Davitt served as the Assistant Pastor of St. Ann's Church in Lenox. But when America declared war on April 6, 1917, he was eager to volunteer. He was first sent to Camp McArthur in Texas and then to France. He not only took care of the pastoral needs of the men in combat—offering Mass, hearing confessions, and administering last rites—but frequently risked his life to rescue wounded soldiers, and was cited for one act of bravery after another. In August 1918, as American forces advanced across Europe against fierce German opposition, and Father Davitt learned that several U.S. troops were trapped in a ravine, he mounted a rescue party, led the doughboys on their escape route, and brought them to safety through heavy gunfire. Under his guidance, the troops did not suffer a single casualty. His own commanding officers, as well as the French military brass, decorated him for valor in battle. Two months later, he was honored again, after jumping up from a fortified trench and running through gunfire to rescue three more trapped American soldiers.

It was his duty to bury the dead and nothing would stop him from fulfilling this mission, even though the Germans kept firing at their enemy during this sacred ceremony. The priest repeatedly risked his own life so that he could give appropriate funerals to those who had fallen in combat. By September 1918, during the Meuse-Argonne offensive, Father Davitt was the chief burial officer for the 5th Corps. He befriended another chaplain, Father Colman O'Flaherty of the 1st Division, who had the same funeral duty as he did. In the midst of one particularly fierce German attack, the two priests made a realistic assessment of their situation and then decided to hear each other's confessions. Their instincts had been right. A few hours later, Father Davitt learned that his brother chaplain had been cut down by artillery fire. For his own actions that day, Father Davitt was recommended for the Distinguished Service Cross.

The Armistice ending World War I was signed at 11 A.M. on the morning of November 11, 1918, but the fighting did not immediately stop. Neither side was certain that the peace was real or would last, so they kept moving forward and discharging rounds. In these final exchanges on the last day of the "War to End All Wars," Father Davitt was performing his daily tasks when he was hit by a stray piece of shrapnel. Newspaper accounts from the next day stated that he had climbed a tree in front of his regiment's headquarters and put up an American flag to celebrate the end of the war. He then climbed down, saluted, and gave a cheer

that the war was over. As he walked away, a shell exploded a few feet from him, killing him instantly. He perished with the soldiers he admired, and with whom he had served so bravely throughout the past year.

His legacy of courage was remembered in many ways back in the United States. In the Arlington, Virginia, National Cemetery, a cenotaph was erected, in memory of the 23 army chaplains who lost their lives in that first world war, and Father Davitt's name was among them. In his home state, his memory is honored by his brother Knights at Fr. William F. Davitt Council 2412 in Lenox, Massachusetts. A VFW post in Chicopee and a town square in Worcester are also named after him. And in Calvary Cemetery in Holyoke, Massachusetts, a monument depicts Father Davitt dressed in uniform and down on his knees, giving care to wounded and dying American soldiers, ignoring the danger all around him.

Knights of Columbus assist an injured soldier at a KC Hut during World War I.

Sergeant Major Daniel Joseph Daly

The United States reluctantly entered World War I, after the carnage had gone on far too long. Americans went into battle not just to fight but to help shape the peace that would follow the end of hostilities. By 1917, millions of French, British, German, and Austrian soldiers had become casualties of trench warfare, in battles more brutal than anyone could have imagined. Americans, including many Catholic men like Dan Daly, of Loyal Council 477 in Middle Village, New York, went to Europe with a strong desire to stop the slaughter, and they promised not to come back until it was "over over there."

Within a year, the war was won and the Americans returned home as heroes. It took a certain kind of courage and bravado to enter someone else's war and bring it to a swift conclusion—and no one possessed more of those qualities than Daly.

Daly was born in Glen Cove, New York, in November of 1873. He seems to have learned how to defend himself at a young age, since there is evidence he was taunted by his peers because he was not tall or muscular. As an adult, he never weighed more than 130 pounds and stood only five feet six inches, but his strength and determination could be seen in his facial features. His jaw was as square as a right angle and put the foundation on a face made for combat. He was one of those soldiers who was every bit as tough as he looked. In January 1899, when he was 26, Daly enlisted in the U.S. Marines and six months later, he was on a ship headed to China to fight against the "Boxers," who got their name from their skill at martial arts, and whose uprising was threatening the lives of foreigners in Peking. There, Daly and his fellow Marines found that the Boxers were especially targeting western and Chinese Christians. During the summer of 1900, when mobs were systematically burning missions and churches (as well as the people inside them) Daly single-handedly held a position under intense enemy fire with only his rifle and bayonet, until reinforcements could arrive. For his actions that day in China, he was awarded his first Congressional Medal of Honor.

Four years later, as a gunnery sergeant, he was sent to Haiti to quell an insurrection in the Caribbean—a perfect assignment for a man of his talents. In the fall of 1904, his company left Fort Liberte for a 6-day reconnaissance mission, and on the evening of October 24, while his detachment was crossing a river, 400 Haitian rebels surrounded the Americans and fired on them from three sides. For the U.S. forces, it appeared to be a hopeless situation. The insurrectionists, known as Cacos, were hiding in bushes and unleashed everything they had at the Marines. Under continuous fire, Daly and his fellow soldiers inched their way forward throughout the long night, taking casualties but never retreating, taking more casualties and gaining ground until they'd secured a favorable position. At daybreak, they charged the Cacos from three angles of their own, surprising and routing the enemy. Gunnery Sergeant Daly led the charge and was once again poised to be a combat hero; for his efforts in Haiti, he would be awarded his second Medal of Honor. Only a handful of Americans had ever achieved this distinction, but Daly wasn't finished.

During World War I, after fighting in the Belleau Wood operations and risking his life by extinguishing a fire in an ammunition dump, he now showed that he had the intelligence to match his courage. Because he'd learned to speak German while growing up on Long Island, he discovered that "laundry day" was approaching for the German enemy—the best time to attack. Daly knew that the Germans would be unprepared for combat that morning, and many would not even be on the front line. When he informed headquarters about this, they ignored him but he had learned to trust his instincts on the battlefield. He led his Marine platoon that day, storming the unsuspecting Germans, who were busy washing their clothes. With automatic pistol in hand and grenades in his belt, Daly single-handedly overtook an enemy machine gun placement and captured or killed the entire crew. Then he carried out a successful assault on a German machine gun nest. For his daring, his intelligence, and the three wounds he took in Europe during the war, he was given the Navy Cross, several Certificates of Merit, the Distinguished Service Cross, the Medaille Militaire, and the Croix de Guerre. Many of those who observed him or fought with him believed that he should have won his third Congressional Medal of Honor but that never happened, for personal reasons. Another famous soldier from World War I, General "Black Jack" Pershing, apparently felt that Daly had been honored enough.

During World War II, a Navy destroyer was named after him. The USS Daly was commissioned in 1943, and saw action throughout the Pacific theater.

Major General John Lejeune, Commandant of the Marine Corps, once called Sergeant Major Dan Daly "the outstanding Marine of all time." Although he only weighed 125 pounds, he remains a giant in the annals of American military history.

The U.S. Navy destroyer USS Daly (DD-519).

Joyce Kilmer

Knights from every walk of life responded to the call when America joined the First World War, from chaplains like Father Davitt to legendary soldiers like Dan Daly (see page 20) to those who ran the "KC Huts" that supported the men in the thick of battle. But none was as unlikely a soldier as Joyce Kilmer, who traded a highly successful career as a poet for the life of a sergeant in the U.S. Army.

Kilmer was born in New Brunswick, New Jersey, on December 6, 1886, and was educated at Rutgers and Columbia. Kilmer was a convert to Catholicism, finding the faith after he married, and he devoted himself to it for the rest of his life. After graduating from Columbia in 1908, he became a magazine and newspaper writer for *The Churchman* and *The New York Times*. He was a good journalist, but his real gift with words lay in the realm of poetry. He had a brilliant ear for the music of language and an insatiable appetite for verse. By 1917, he'd gained recognition as one of America's leading poets. His 1913 poem "Trees" was his best-known, and was widely anthologized. His published volumes were critically acclaimed and sold well. As a successful man of letters, and as a husband with four children and a pregnant wife (the poet Aline Murray), Kilmer had everything to look forward to. His life was full and his career had taken off. He was as admired among the nation's poetry lovers as he was by his fellow Knights of Columbus, whom he'd joined several years earlier at Council 1177 in Suffern, New York (later, in 1917, he transferred to New Rochelle Council 339).

The Order stressed patriotism, and as soon as the Lusitania was sunk by a German U-boat in the Atlantic, and the United States aligned itself with the Allies in World War I, Kilmer embraced that principle without hesitation. Well over draft age, he enlisted in the Seventh New York National Guard regiment just days after the Lusitania incident, and was soon transferred to the Headquarters Company of the 165th Infantry. Leaving behind a lucrative career as a speaker and writer, he prepared to say goodbye to his wife and children, one of whom died just as he was preparing to go abroad. This tragedy might have deterred another man, but not Kilmer. As a sergeant in the United States Army, the poet sailed for France and threw himself into soldiering. The harsher the conditions, the more cheerful he seemed to be. He was often described as wearing a brooding look that went away as soon as the fighting started. On the front lines, the burden of his thoughts and emotions lifted, as he had more immediate things to confront. Kilmer came alive in combat in ways that nobody could have foreseen. And his Catholic faith was never more evident than when he was facing battle.

"I have had very little chance to read contemporary poetry out here," he wrote from a trench in France in 1918, "but I hope that it is reflecting the virtues which are blossoming on the blood-soaked soil of this land—courage, self-abnegation, love and faith—not faith in some abstract goodness, but faith in God and His Son and in the Holy Ghost and in the Church which God Himself founded and still rules. France has turned to her ancient faith with more passionate devotion than she has shown for centuries. I believe America is learning the same lesson from the war and is cleansing herself of the cynicism, pessimism, materialism and lust for novelty which has hampered our national development."

Night after night, he would leave his trench and crawl through dirt and barbed-wire fences in the darkness in order to locate the positions of German guns. In the morning, he would return to his superior officers with valuable intelligence

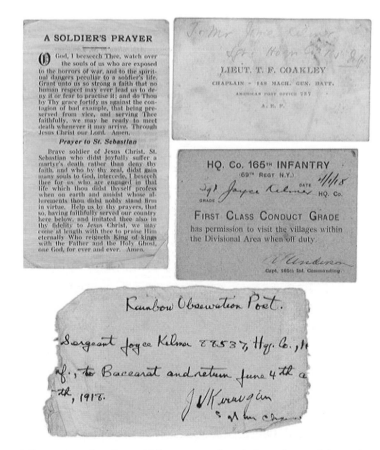

The papers that Joyce Kilmer carried with him during his service in World War I.

about enemy deployments—often with his flesh scratched and his clothing torn to shreds. The courage he'd once displayed with the pen, in searching out and writing about his inner life, was now being displayed on the public stage of international warfare. He actively sought the most dangerous assignments, no matter where they took him and regardless of the risks. With intelligence information that he helped to provide, Allied forces launched the Battle of Ourcq on July 27, 1918, and three days later, after his regiment had been ravaged by casualties, Kilmer volunteered for combat. The battalion commander sent him out to lead a patrol to find the exact location of enemy armaments hidden in the woods.

Hours later, as the battalion advanced, a couple of soldiers spotted Kilmer lying on the ground with his eyes open. Approaching him slowly, they realized that he had a bullet hole in his head and was lifeless. One of America's greatest poets had died on the field of battle, not yet 32 years of age. He was buried in France's Oise-Aisne Cemetery; the French government awarded him the Croix de Guerre for bravery.

One of Kilmer's last works, "Prayer of a Soldier," came out of his experience in France. Every word revealed the faith he'd lived when writing poetry and fighting in a war:

> My shoulders ache beneath my pack
> (Lie easier, Cross, upon His back).
>
> I march with feet that burn and smart
> (Tread, Holy Feet, upon my heart).
>
> Men shout at me who may not speak
> (They scourged Thy back and smote Thy cheek).
>
> I may not lift a hand to clear
> My eyes of salty drops that sear.
>
> (Then shall my fickle soul forget
> Thy agony of Bloody Sweat?)
>
> My rifle hand is stiff and numb
> (From Thy pierced palm red rivers come).
>
> Lord, Thou didst suffer more for me
> Than all the hosts of land and sea.
>
> So let me render back again
> This millionth of Thy gift. Amen.

23

Dr. Claude Brown

In World War I, the Knights of Columbus brought the concept of "KC Huts" to Europe's front lines. The Order opened these relief centers for members of the American Expeditionary Force overseas and near training centers stateside. They were a place where soldiers could get away from the fighting and pick up goods that were often in short supply, such as a hot cup of coffee or a blanket. The atmosphere was friendly and relaxed, no money was needed—the motto was "everyone welcome, everything free"—and the huts provided the soldiers with a kind of

home away from home. The Knights had offered the same sort of support to U.S. soldiers on a limited scale during border skirmishes with Mexico in 1916, but World War I was a major, large-scale effort, infinitely greater in its cost and complexity. The KC Huts in the European theater won praise around the world.

When the United States entered World War II in December 1941, the support for American soldiers that had been provided by the KC Huts in the "Great War" was assigned this time around to the new United Service Organization (USO), and Supreme Knight Francis Matthews become the Catholic Church's representative at the USO. In the Philippines, Knights set up a KC Hut program that served American and Filipino soldiers until the fall of Manila to the Japanese in 1942, and again after they were finally driven out in 1945.

Canada, a member of the British Commonwealth, became involved in World War II more than two years earlier than the United States, as soon as war was declared in Europe in September 1939. Dr. Claude Brown, a Canadian dentist who'd served with distinction as a lieutenant colonel in World War I, had seen firsthand the value of the huts, and within ten days of the outbreak of World War II, he had formed a committee to set up a Canadian Knights of Columbus Hut program.

Brown was born in London, Ontario, in 1877 and graduated from the Royal College of Dental Surgeons in Toronto. During World War I, he'd worked at a field hospital of the Royal Canadian Army Medical Corps, saw action in the Gallipoli campaign, and had been awarded the Order of the British Empire. After returning to his dental practice, Dr. Brown became a member of the Board of Governors at the University of Western Ontario. He was very active in the Knights of Columbus, serving as Grand Knight of London Council, District Deputy (1920–23), State Deputy of Ontario (1923–25), and as a Supreme Director of the

Order (1926–41). He was a modest man, quiet to a fault, but uncompromising in fulfilling his duty to others—a natural leader in everything he joined. His particular interest was sports, and he worked with both the University of Ontario and the Knights to support athletic activities.

In 1939 Dr. Brown assumed the title of President of the Knights of Columbus Canadian Army Huts and was joined in the effort to organize the program by a number of Canadian officers of the Knights, including the state deputies of Ontario and Quebec. The effort was headquartered in the Canadian capital of Ottawa, and during its first six months in operation, the Knights raised almost $230,000 for the effort. Soon there were Knights of Columbus hostels and morale programs near training camps in Nova Scotia, New Brunswick, and Newfoundland as well as recreation centers in the large cities.

In May 1940, Dr. Brown sailed for England to set up KC Huts where British Commonwealth servicemen on furlough could take advantage of their hospitality and entertainment. "In establishing the Knights of Columbus Canadian Army Huts, in order to assist in the maintenance of morale among the Canadian Forces in Canada and overseas," he wrote to his fellow citizens on January 1, 1941, "the Knights of Columbus are continuing the work carried on by them in the Great War. In England at the present time, I am supervising the work of fourteen representatives of the organization. We are not operating in any of the cities or towns, but we may be found with the men in the lines and the barracks, and where the soldier reads 'K. of C. War Services' he knows, irrespective of his race or creed, he will be welcomed and will find everything free."

A few months later after writing his message to the citizens of Canada, Dr. Brown was injured during an air raid on London. He was supposed to return to Canada for rest and convalescence but instead he went on to Glasgow, Scotland, to continue working on the Huts project. On May 15, 1941, Lt. Colonel Brown died in Glasgow from his war wounds. He was buried at the Canadian Military Cemetery in London, England. His absence was felt everywhere that he'd served and everywhere the huts had been established. His death made those left behind more committed to carrying

out his plan of helping soldiers cope in wartime, while staying in touch with the roots of their faith. The work that Brown had begun was carried on by thousands of his brother Knights. And in addition to setting up and operating the huts, Canadian Knights (rather than the government) provided all chapel supplies for Catholic chaplains in the Canadian armed forces, including stations of the cross, kneeling benches, statues, rosaries and prayer books. With the invasion of France in June 1944, Canadian KC Huts were soon established on the continent as well.

In 1951, a decade after his death, the Dr. Claude Brown Memorial Trophy was formally presented to the University of Western Ontario by a group of his friends who wanted to honor him. The trophy had been cast by the noted English silversmith, Dunstan Pruden, and would be presented annually to the student who'd made the greatest contribution to the school's sports team and who stood for the professional and spiritual ideals embodied by Dr. Brown. For posterity, Claude Brown's name would be associated with a peacetime activity, but he will always be remembered most for his wartime service in helping those who had sacrificed their safety and often their lives the cause of freedom, just as he himself had done.

Knights of Columbus Supervisors guard the casket of Dr. Brown.

Father John B. DeValles

In August 1879, John B. DeValles was born in San Miguel, Azores, and came to the United States at two years old with his family, who settled in New Bedford, Massachusetts. He graduated from New Bedford High School and made plans to join the priesthood. After attending St. Charles College in Baltimore, he then entered the seminary in Montreal. He was ordained as a priest in mid-June 1906, celebrating his first Mass in Fall River, Massachusetts, at St. Mary's Church, on June 21,1906. Father DeValles served at Our Lady of Mt. Carmel Church and then as pastor of St. John the Baptist Church in New Bedford. He had been a brilliant student, and he was fluent in six languages, which helped him in his priestly duties. He opened the first Portuguese parochial school in America and was planning to

start others, but his life was about to change forever, when he answered the call to serve his Church and his country during "The Great War." He would soon became known in America and abroad as "a man of peace in a time of war."

In September 1917, he was appointed a Knights of Columbus chaplain with the 104th Regiment of the 26th Division of the U.S. infantry—known as the "Yankee Division" because it was made up of National Guardsmen from throughout New England. The following year, after the United States entry into World War I, he was made a chaplain in the America Expeditionary Force with the rank of first lieutenant. He accompanied the doughboys to Europe and spent months providing them with the sacraments and ministering to the wounded in "no man's land," that bloody strip of land between the German and Allied forces where so many lost their lives. Father DeValles's division sailed for Europe with 28,000 men. By war's end the division had suffered 11,995 casualties and 1,739 dead.

It wasn't just the priest's courage that stood out on the fields of battle, but his eagerness to make life better for those sacrificing everything for the war. As American troops hunkered down in the trenches and prepared to hold off the German attacks, Father DeValles put up a wooden sign near a dugout right next to an active combat sector. In crude letters, it read "Father John's office," and a steady stream of men found their way inside. Within these dirt walls, he ministered to the soldiers' needs, which encompassed everything from the very public difficulties of fighting a war to the most private aspects of their personal lives. They could ask him anything, and he would listen and offer counsel, advice, and comfort. He was not only a priest, but a man in harm's way every day, just as they were. He knew their dreams and their deepest fears because he lived among them and asked for no special protection from the enemy.

Through his influence, he was able to organize a minstrel show for the troops—after the soldiers had captured an upright piano from a high-ranking German officer. The Americans hauled the piano everywhere the regiment traveled, so that the men could have a break from the rigors of trench warfare and relax with singing and music. What might seem like a small thing in most circumstances could make all the difference to those facing death on a daily basis.

Father DeValles's main job on the front lines was searching for wounded and dying soldiers. When he found them, he served them, whether they were German or American troops. His duties and compassion were not limited to one side; anyone caught in this nightmare of violence would get all the support he could provide. On many occasions, he exposed himself to heavy artillery and machine-gun fire in order to carry out his ministry and assist in the removal of the wounded. His actions became the stuff of combat lore. In *The Knights of Columbus in Peace and War*, authors Maurice Francis Egan and John B. Kennedy wrote of one soldier's experience of the priest's wartime heroism: "…he had seen Father DeValles at an advanced dressing station staggering through sheer fatigue with a stretcher bound to his wrists with wire, the wire cutting through the flesh to the bone, carrying in the wounded hour after hour."

When he didn't return to the trenches one day, searchers located him in a heap on the ground, unconscious and lying next to a dead soldier he'd been trying to help. They dragged him to safety and tried to nurse him back to health, but he never fully recovered and gradually began to deteriorate. In 1919, Father DeValles came home but once again he spent much of his time with the sick, this time as a patient. As he lay dying, the news that he had won an award for his battlefield bravery was slowly making its way by messenger from Washington, D.C. It arrived a half hour before he died; he awoke briefly from a coma, and was informed by his nurse that he had won the Distinguished Service Cross. Tears filled his eyes when he learned of this honor, but sadly, he soon slipped back into unconsciousness and died on May 12, 1920, at age 41. For caring for others under fire, he had already received France's Croix de Guerre for his bravery at Apremont while he was overseas. And while he did not live to see the Distinguished Service Cross arrive from Washington, his friends derived some comfort from the fact that at least he

knew he had won it. Father DeValles was given full military honors at his funeral, with tributes from local and national leaders. Awarded a hero's burial, he was memorialized as the "Angel of the Trenches." Following his death, many of his wartime artifacts and medals were placed in the Knights of Columbus Museum in New Haven, so that visitors could see them and appreciate his valor. The museum loaned the artifacts to the Museum of Our National Heritage in Lexington, Massachusetts, for its celebrated exhibit "Over There: The Yankee Division in World War I." People who came could look at pictures of Father John and learn of his sacrifices and those of so many others during the war. On display were both sides of "New Bedford's Fighting Chaplain"—the soldier and the priest. Today his memory is kept alive in his hometown of New Bedford, where an elementary school bears his name. Given his love of education, it is a fitting tribute.

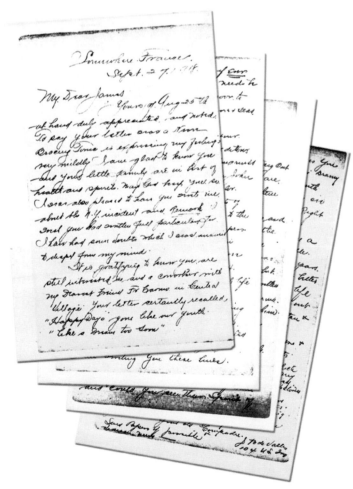

A letter that Father DeValles wrote from the trenches of World War I, September 27, 1918.

CHAPTER THREE

The 1920s

George Herman "Babe" Ruth

The lives of many disadvantaged Americans have been shaped and recast in Catholic schools and orphanages. The most inspirational story of them all concerns a youngster who got his second chance at a Catholic reformatory in Baltimore, where he was pulled back from the edge of what otherwise would have been a tragic, wasted life, and put instead on a path to success he could never have imagined.

Born in 1895, George Ruth was the first child of a saloon-keeper and his wife. Both his father and mother worked long hours at the saloon, barely making enough to survive. George, meanwhile, grew up on the tough streets of Baltimore. By the time he was seven his parents had decided send him to St. Mary's Industrial School for Boys, an institution for orphans and delinquents. His father signed over custody of his son to the Catholic order of Xaverian Brothers, and George rarely ever saw his parents after that.

George, a difficult, "incorrigible" child, came under the thumb of the school's Prefect of Discipline. Brother Matthias was a large, muscular man who taught the boys at St. Mary's about sports and about getting control of themselves on and off the playing field. "Coach" Matthias took a special interest in George, because in spite of difficulties, he was a likable boy with obvious athletic skills.

The structure and discipline that George had never known at home were now in place for the first time in his life. He received religious instruction and was exposed to organized sports. Brother Matthias showed him how to throw a baseball with speed and how to hit one with power. He worked patiently with George to sharpen his talents and encouraged him to take the game seriously. By the age of 15, young Ruth had become a standout pitcher whose reputation was spreading to Baltimore's other parochial schools.

Later in life, Ruth described Brother Matthias as "the greatest man I've ever known. He was the father I needed. He taught me to read and write—and taught me the difference between right and wrong."

In 1914, on Brother Matthias's recommendation, Ruth got a tryout with the Baltimore Orioles and signed a contract. Jack Dunn, owner and manager of the Orioles, was known for finding and developing young players and when Ruth arrived, the other Orioles began calling him "Jack's newest babe." The seed of a legend had been planted and George had the talent to make it grow. The next year Dunn sold him to the Boston Red Sox for $2,900.

Within months, Babe Ruth was pitching brilliantly for the Red Sox. In 1916, he won a World Series game against Brooklyn and in 1918 he won two more versus the Chicago Cubs, while setting a Series record by throwing 29 scoreless innings. In spite of these numbers, he was such a potent slugger that the Red Sox switched him to the outfield so he could play every day. In 1919 (the year he joined the Knights of Columbus), he hit 29 home runs, breaking the major league record held by Gabby Kraveth. Baseball had seen great hitters and great pitchers, but until now nobody had never been able to do both at the highest levels of the game. Following the 1919 season, the Red Sox were strapped for cash and sold Ruth to the New York Yankees.

In 1920, confidence in the game of baseball was at an all-time low following the infamous Black Sox gambling scandal. Many people felt that baseball would never recover. The game badly needed a lift and a new hero, and Babe Ruth was there to give it one. In 1920, he hit 54 home runs, nearly doubling his previous record, and wherever he traveled to take his swings at home plate, fans showed up to watch him. His popularity soon reached an all-time high and he was instrumental in reestablishing baseball as the great American pastime.

In 1923, led by the Babe, the Yankees won their first World Series. He'd become such an attraction in New York that the team was able to construct its own ballpark, officially known as Yankee Stadium, but everyone called it "The House That Ruth Built." (Ruth would have enjoyed knowing that after his death, it could also have been called "The House the Knights Owned," since the Knights of Columbus bought the land on which the stadium was located as an investment in 1953 and owned it for several decades.) In 1927, Babe set the immortal record of 60 home runs in a 154-game season, and when he retired in 1935, he'd hit 714 round-trippers. By then, Ruth had led the Yankees to seven American League championships and four World Series titles, and the Yanks were on their way to becoming the most renowned franchise in sports history.

Apart from Babe's Hall of Fame numbers, he lived a huge public life. The Xaverian Brothers had taught him the value of faith and inspired him to help disadvantaged children just as he'd been given a hand when he needed it. Since Ruth himself had grown up without a family, he was particularly sensitive to orphans and visited them all over the nation. He dropped in on hospitals and reformatories from coast to coast and always had time for those who most needed his inspiration. He gave away mementos, which children treasured for years. While talking to sick boys and girls, he might ask if they wanted him to hit a home run for them. On more than one occasion, after they'd answered yes, he'd go out and fulfill their wishes.

Ruth had become active in the Knights of Columbus when he was still playing for the Red Sox in 1919, joining Père Marquette Council 271 in South Boston. In 1921, Babe was on hand to receive the ceremonial first brick for the construction of the Knights' $2,000,000 New York welfare center.

After his retirement, he traveled extensively, visiting orphanages and hospitals wherever he went. A year before he died from cancer, he established and endowed the Babe Ruth Foundation for destitute children. He was given the last rites of the Catholic Church in July 1948, and Father Thomas Kaufman was with him when he died a month later. "The Babe said his prayers to the very end," Father Kaufman said later. "He received all the last rites and he died a good Catholic." After his death on August 16, more than 100,000 fans came to pay their respects as his body lay in state at Yankee Stadium. Thousands more surrounded St. Patrick's Cathedral while Cardinal Spellman presided at the Babe's Requiem Mass. Among those attending his funeral was "Mr. Baseball," fellow Knight of Columbus Connie Mack (see page 14).

For nearly three decades, Babe Ruth personified "The Golden Age of Sports." He enriched not just baseball, but the entire nation. It's hard to conceive of America in the 20th century without Babe Ruth. And just as his impact on baseball would live on, so would his dedication to charity, the first principle of the Knights of Columbus, on behalf of children, especially poor children, everywhere.

Babe Ruth visited sick children at the Knickerbocker Hospital in New York, April 15, 1930.

The Mexican Martyrs

Father Luis Batis Sainz was shot by a firing squad on August 15, 1926.

The 1920s brought a revolution to Mexico, along with the widespread persecution of Catholics. Missionaries were expelled from the country, Catholic seminaries and schools were closed, and the Church was forbidden to own property. Priests and laymen were told to denounce Jesus and their faith in public; if they refused, they faced not just punishment but torture and death. During this time of oppression and cruelty, the Knights of Columbus did not retreat in Mexico but grew dramatically, from 400 members in 1918 to 43 councils and 6,000 members just five years later. In the United States at the time, the Knights handed out 5 million pamphlets that described the brutality of the Mexican government toward Catholics. As a result, the

Mexican government greatly feared and eventually outlawed the Order.

Thousands of men, many of whom were Knights, would not bow to these threats or renounce their faith, and they often paid with their lives. They took a stand when that was the most difficult thing they could do, and their courage and devotion should never be forgotten. Here are some of the stories of the Knights of Columbus who joined the ranks of the Mexican Martyrs and were among the 25 victims of religious persecution canonized in 2000 by Pope John Paul II.

Father Luis Batiz Sainz was born in 1870, and was a member of Council 2367. On August 15, 1926, at Chalchihuites, Zacatecas, he and three laymen—David Roldan, who was only nineteen at the time, Salvador Lara,

Father José María Robles Hurtado was martyred on June 25, 1927.

and Manuel Morales, were lined up in front of a firing squad for refusing to submit to President Plutarco Elias Calles's anti-religious laws. When Father Batiz Sainz asked the soldiers to free one of the captives, Manuel Morales, who had sons and daughters, Morales wouldn't hear of it.

"I am dying for God," he declared, "and God will care for my children."

Smiling, Father Sainz gave his friend absolution and said: "See you in heaven."

Father José María Robles Hurtado was a member of Council 1979. Ordained in 1913, he founded the Sisters of the Sacred Heart of Jesus in Guadalajara when he was only twenty-five. On June 25, 1927, he was arrested while

Father Miguel de la Mora was shot as he prayed the rosary on August 7, 1927.

preparing to celebrate Mass. Early the next morning, he was hanged from an oak tree, but not before he had forgiven his murderers and offered a prayer for his parish. He went so far as to place the rope around his own neck, so that none of his captors would hold the title of murderer.

That same year, Father Mateo Correa Megallanes, who was a member of Council 2140, was arrested and taken to Durango. While in prison, he was ordered by the commanding officer on February 5, 1927, to hear the confessions of his fellow prisoners. Then the commander demanded to know what they had told him. Of course, Father Correa Megallanes wouldn't violate the seal of confession, and so, the next day, he was taken to a local cemetery and executed by the soldiers.

Father Miguel de la Mora of Colima also belonged to Council 2140. Along with several other priests, he publicly

Father Mateo Correa Megallanes was shot on February 6, 1927.

signed a letter opposing the anti-religious laws imposed by the government. He was soon arrested and, with his brother Regino looking on, Father de la Mora was executed without a trial by a single shot from a military officer as he prayed his rosary. It was August 7, 1927.

Two months later, Father Rodrigo Aguilar Alemán of Unión de Tula in Jalisco, and a member of Council 2330, met a similar fate. Rather than escape when the soldiers arrived, Father Alemán remained at the seminary to burn the list of seminary students, and thus protect them from being known. When the soldiers demanded his identity, he told them only that he was a priest. He was taken to the main square of Ejutla, where the seminary was located. He publicly forgave his killers, and then a soldier gave him

Father Pedro de Jesús Maldonado Lucero was brutally beaten on Ash Wednesday 1937 and died the next day.

the chance to save himself by giving the "right" answer to this question, "Who lives?"

Father Aguilar Alemán would be spared if he simply said, "Long live the supreme government."

But he replied, "Christ the King and Our Lady of Guadalupe." The noose that had been secured to a mango tree was tightened, then relaxed twice. Each time it was relaxed, he was asked the same question and each time he gave the same response. The third time the noose was tightened, he died.

Father Pedro de Jesús Maldonado Lucero was a member of Council 2419. Forced to study for the priesthood in El Paso, Texas, because of the political situation in Mexico, he

Father Rodrigo Aguilar Alemán was ordained in 1905.

returned home after his ordination in 1918 despite the risk. Captured on Ash Wednesday, 1937, while distributing ashes to the faithful, Father Maldonado Lucero was so savagely beaten that one eye was forced from its socket. He died the next day at a local hospital. His tombstone aptly described this martyr in four words: "You are a priest."

Two other Knights have been declared martyrs by the Vatican in 2004, which has cleared the way for their beatification. They are Servants of God, José Trinidad Rangel Montaño, a diocesan priest from León and member of Council 2484, and Claretian Father Andres Sola Molist, a Spaniard, and member of Council 1963. They were executed for their faith in Rancho de San Joaquin, Mexico, in April 1927.

These men, and many thousands more, paid the ultimate sacrifice for their Catholic activities in Mexico during the 1920s and 1930s. But throughout that period, the Knights of Columbus in Mexico kept the faith and hundreds gave their lives to protect their beliefs, some as martyrs and others in the armed Cristero struggle against the government.

Though he always advocated peaceful resistance, Pope Pius XI singled out the Knights of Columbus for praise in his 1926 encyclical *Iniquis Afflictisque*, writing, "First of all we mention the Knights of Columbus, an organization which is found in all states of the Mexican Republic and fortunately is made up of active and industrious members who, because of their practical lives and open profession of the Faith, as well as by their zeal in assisting the Church, have brought great honor upon themselves."

The Knights and the Church at large in Mexico were consistently supported by the Knights in the United States, who, in addition to distributing literature that informed the American people of the plight of the Church in Mexico, also lobbied President Coolidge to bring pressure to end the persecution. In 1926, President Coolidge met with a Knights of Columbus delegation made up of, among others, Supreme Knight James Flaherty, as well as future Supreme Knight Luke Hart, and Supreme Director William Prout (see page 6). President Coolidge affirmed his administration's commitment to bringing about a resolution to the problems in Mexico.

Though the Knights had been outlawed in Mexico, with hundreds killed, and even *Columbia* magazine banned by the Mexican postal service for a time, the Knights of Columbus survived. In 2005, 100 years after the first council in Mexico was formed, the anniversary was commemorated by a nationwide tour throughout Mexico of the relics of the Mexican martyrs that were given to the Knights of Columbus in 2001. At the centennial convention in Mexico City, Supreme Knight Carl Anderson declared that the Knights of Mexico are "second to none" in their devotion to "our founding ideals and their devotion to the Catholic faith."

Father Michael J. Ahern, S.J.

The Knights of Columbus have a long history of teaching tolerance, as exemplified by the work of Edward F. McSweeney (see page 8), who led a historical commission that published monographs on the achievements of Jews, African Americans, and others. One Knight who shared McSweeney's vision and worked hard to promote it was Father Michael J. Ahern, a member of Crusader Council 2706 of the Knights of Columbus in Worcester, Massachusetts.

Born in New York City on May 25, 1877, Michael learned religious tolerance at a very young age. He was raised in a neighborhood where people from various religious backgrounds all lived near one another. Eventually, becoming an accomplished priest, he spoke in 1929 at Harvard, where he recalled two of his closest boyhood friends. "Johnny went to the Lutheran Church... Jakey to the Synagogue, and I went to the Jesuit church. No one of us ever discussed or questioned the right of the other to go to his own church— it never entered our minds."

The tolerant attitude that Father Ahern learned as a child was reflected in his work throughout his life. But first Father Ahern became known for his research in science. Father Ahern believed that science and religion were not incompatible, as he would explain many times during his distinguished academic career. Having received a master's degree from Woodstock College, a Jesuit institution near Baltimore, Maryland, he began teaching chemistry and biology at Boston College in 1902. By 1911, he became head of the Chemistry and Geology department at Canisius College in Buffalo. By 1925, Father Ahern was named head of the department of Geology and Chemistry at Weston College, where he remained for the next several decades. The research he conducted in climatology and seismology became internationally known, and by 1940, he was named the director of the Weston Observatory, which monitors the Northeast for possible earthquake activity. Father Ahern was a fellow of the American Association for the Advancement of Science, and he also earned a number of awards and honorary degrees.

A true Renaissance man, Father Ahern also enjoyed a career in radio. It was his many years as a broadcaster that won him friends from all over the eastern United States. Father Ahern found in the new medium of radio the perfect outlet to discuss what mattered most to him: his respect for other religions, his love of science, and his devotion to the Catholic faith. While today it is not unusual for people of diverse religions to meet and study together, it was far less common in the 1920s, making it more difficult to challenge misconceptions and stereotypes. But thanks to radio, listeners could not only hear sermons by members of their own religion, but learn about other religions, as well. In Boston, there were several stations that invited priests, rabbis, and ministers to give short inspirational talks and answer questions from listeners. Father Ahern made several appearances in this capacity during the mid-1920s and was very well received.

Given his reputation as an educator and his ability to explain Catholic teachings on the radio, it is not surprising that Cardinal O'Connell in Boston requested that Father Ahern lead a group of Catholic clergy and laymen who would produce a weekly radio program about Catholicism. It was called the Catholic Truth Period, and its first broadcast was in the fall of 1929 on station WNAC. Unlike the typical church service, this program featured not only theology but entertainment—music from some of the area's best-known Catholic choirs and vocalists. Father Ahern hosted a segment called the Question Box, during which listeners could send in their queries about Catholic beliefs and doctrines. He also gave a series of educational talks, including several on science and religion. He was determined to help both Catholics and non-Catholics understand that being a scientist did not in any way mean one could not be a person of faith, and he also was determined to handle other misconceptions the public had about Catholic beliefs.

Meanwhile, also on station WNAC, Rabbi Harry Levi of Boston's Temple Israel was doing broadcasts aimed at Jewish listeners and finding the same phenomenon that Father Ahern found: listeners were not just from his religion, and many of their questions reflected a lack of understanding about what Jews believed. It did not take long for Rabbi Levi and Father Ahern to become friends, since both shared a desire to teach tolerance and actively combat prejudice. In November of 1929, Rabbi Levi and Father Ahern were part of an interfaith conference, the Calvert Roundtable at Harvard. It would be one of many occasions when they would give talks and seminars. Their speeches received newspaper coverage, and throughout the 1930s, both men led by example, frequently sharing a podium to speak about the importance of interfaith dialogue and cooperation. And Father Ahern even took it one step further: in 1936 he went

on a six-week trip across the United States, along with a Baltimore rabbi, Morris Lazaron, and a New York minister, Dr. Everett Clinchy, on what the three called a "pilgrimage of neighborliness" to promote tolerance. The three spoke at colleges and civic organizations and met with community leaders. Dr. Clinchy was also the founder of the National Conference of Jews and Christians and Father Ahern was an active participant as well as a member of its executive committee. In fact, he was a delegate to an international conference on religious tolerance in 1946.

For 21 years, New England Catholics became accustomed to spending a part of their Sunday listening to Father Ahern's Catholic Truth Period. When he finally resigned from doing the program, it was due to ill health. He died on June 5, 1951, and his popularity was such that several Boston newspapers put the news on page 1. A pontifical funeral mass was offered by Bishop Eric F. MacKenzie, and among the 2,000 in attendance was John E. Swift, Supreme Knight of the Order. He too had been involved with radio and understood the important work Father Ahern had done as well as the example he had set. As Boston's Catholic newspaper, the Pilot, wrote, Father Michael J. Ahern was "a good and faithful servant...and outstanding example of gentlemanliness and scholarship...[who] shared his wisdom with the young and his strength with the weak."

Father Ahern (left) and Rabbi Levi (center) are honored by the National Council of Christians and Jews, led by John Ratcliffe (right), Boston, 1938.

Alfred E. Smith

Mexico wasn't the only place where anti-Catholic prejudice was flourishing in the 1920s. It was very much alive in the United States as well. Urged on by the Ku Klux Klan, in 1922 Oregon voters approved an initiative aimed directly at Catholic parochial schools, requiring that all children attend public schools. The Knights of Columbus quickly provided funds for a Supreme Court challenge, and the law was declared unconstitutional. But the most virulent prejudice of the decade awaited New York's popular Irish-American Governor, Al Smith.

Smith was known as the "Happy Warrior" because he loved the passionate engagement, the give and take, the rough and tumble environment of American politics. He was born on December 30, 1873, on New York's lower east side, and as a boy he went to work selling newspapers on street corners. He aspired to complete high school and go on to

college, but when Al was 13, his father suddenly died, and that marked the end of the adolescent's formal education. He had to support his family now, which he did by putting in long hours at the Fulton Fish Market.

Throughout Smith's political career, he emphasized his early experience in speeches, and identified most closely with people who made a living with their hands. These things, combined with his spiritual foundation in the Church and his longstanding connection to the Knights of Columbus (he was a lifelong member of Dr. John G. Coyle Council 163 in New York City), molded his ambitions, values, and empathy with the underdog.

In 1903, he won a seat in the New York State Assembly. Painfully aware of his humble background and lack of education, he stayed up night after night to research and study the bills that crossed his desk. He made up for his lack of book learning by his natural flair for public speaking. He intuitively knew what mattered to most Americans and how to connect with it—quickly and concisely—through language. The ability to think and talk on his feet soon elevated him to majority leader in the Assembly.

In 1911, following the horrific Triangle Shirtwaist Company fire in New York City, Smith became vice-chairman of the commission appointed to investigate the troubling factory conditions throughout New York. He developed recommendations for improving the sweatshops where many poor immigrants were forced to work, and he wrote safety legislation to protect laborers from dangers on the job. The Tammany Hall political machine had given Smith an assist when he was first running for office, but he now stood in opposition to its corruption and greed, much to the bosses' dismay.

After leaving the Assembly, he became sheriff of New York County in 1915, and then won election as Governor of New York in 1918, a victory few had expected him to attain. He proved to be very popular with voters, and served four terms as chief executive in Albany, building a national reputation.

In 1924, he sought the Democratic presidential nod, and Franklin D. Roosevelt delivered his nomination speech, calling Smith "the Happy Warrior of the political battlefield." But the convention deadlocked, and on the 103rd ballot, after nine days of infighting, they chose a little-known lawyer named John Davis, who lost in a landslide. By 1928, Smith was the favorite for his party's nomination, and delegates to the Democratic national convention in Houston selected him on the very first ballot. By then, there were many Catholic officeholders at the state and local level, but this election would reveal whether 1920s' America was finally ready for a Catholic president.

Smith had a lot going for him, including the staunch support of both Franklin and Eleanor Roosevelt. But anti-Catholic sentiment proved to be deeply ingrained in American life. The Ku Klux Klan, which hated Catholics as well as Jews and African Americans, charged that "A Vote for Al Smith Is a Vote for the Pope." Smith decided to tackle the issue head-on, and scheduled a major speech in Oklahoma City on religious intolerance. The KKK saw to it that burning crosses greeted him as his train rolled into town. The following night, an anti-Catholic evangelist named John Roach Straton rented the same hall and delivered a screed entitled "Al Smith and the Forces of Hell."

As bizarre as it may seem today, there were many who were certain that if Smith was elected president, Protestant children would be forced to attend Catholic schools and the Pope would take up residence in the White House. Smith got only 41 percent of the vote and even lost his own state of New York, although he carried a dozen of the country's largest cities. In 1928, the United States wasn't ready to elect a Catholic president. One joke going around after the election was that Smith had sent the pope a one-word telegram: "Unpack!"

As Smith was losing the presidential race, Roosevelt was winning the right to replace him as governor of New York. In 1932, they both sought the Democratic presidential nomination and Roosevelt emerged the victor. The bitter loss to a former ally ended Smith's long and distinguished political career, and Smith found himself persona non grata at the White House.

When he died in October 1944, his memorial service was attended by Eleanor Roosevelt, but not FDR. By then, the employee benefit legislation he'd pioneered in New York in the 1920s had been adopted by most other states. But Al Smith had cleared the path for more than social legislation. A few months before Smith's death, a young Navy Lieutenant named John F. Kennedy narrowly escaped an encounter with a Japanese destroyer in the South Pacific. In 1960, 16 years after Smith's funeral, the United States was finally ready for a Catholic president, and Kennedy was sent to the White House. Like Smith, Kennedy was a Catholic and a Knight, and he owed a great deal to the Happy Warrior who paved the way.

Al Smith (right) during a train trip to promote his campaign for the presidency, circa 1928.

John Edward Reagan

Reagan family Christmas card, circa 1916–1917. Left to right: John, Neil, Ronald, and Nelle Reagan.

John Reagan's son didn't follow in his father's steps as a Knight of Columbus himself, but his life was touched deeply by the Order. Several times during his eight years in the Oval Office, President Reagan spoke to the Knights and always offered the same story.

"I want to tell you," the President said in a 1986 speech in Chicago, "that I've had a place in my heart for the Knights of Columbus since I was a boy. You see, my father was a Knight, and he never missed an opportunity to express his pride in the K. of C. or join in its efforts on behalf of charity

and tolerance. I can still remember when the silent picture, *Birth of a Nation*, opened in our hometown. Dad told us that the movie portrayed the Ku Klux Klan in a favorable light, and that the Reagans were one family that wouldn't be seeing it. Even as a boy, I sensed that in taking that stand my father had done something strong and good, something noble. To this day, I have never seen that famous movie."

Little is known about John Edward Reagan's years with the Order, except through the words of his son. We do know that he worked as a shoe salesman in northwestern Illinois, finally settling in the town of Dixon, where the future president attended high school. While Ronald's mother Nelle was a Protestant, he was profoundly influenced by his father's love for the Catholic faith. John Edward Reagan died of heart failure in May 1941. Like many other men, the older Reagan served the Knights and his community diligently and quietly without expecting to come into the spotlight. He let his actions testify to his convictions and principles, and he worked to hand down his beliefs to the next generation. What is known about J.R. Reagan is that he conveyed to his son the same values that he found in the Knights of Columbus. Those values were evident whenever Ronald Reagan talked to the Knights or spoke about the Order in public, and they could also be heard when the president addressed the nation. His father's faith and belief in serving others always came through. That is why President Reagan's speeches to the Knights of Columbus were so notable and heartfelt, and worth quoting at length. They stand as a tribute to his father's memory.

"All that you do as Knights of Columbus," the President once said, "arises from the fundamental values you hold so dear—your belief in a just and loving God, in the validity of hard work, in the central importance of the family. When I talked about these fundamental values myself during the campaign of 1980, there was a certain amount of questioning, even criticism. Then came the campaign of 1984, and I know you must have been as gratified as I was to hear both sides talking about values like neighborhood and family. But it was the Knights who led the way, stressing the importance of fundamental values long before you were joined by me or any other politician…

"As important as your works of charity are, however, you have also maintained individually and corporately your stalwart faith in religious and family values. Through activities such as the Catholic Information Service, you've stood unhesitatingly for these values. And that's why, for example, you were earnestly working for an end to racial and ethnic prejudice in America, fighting for justice for Blacks and Jews as well as for Catholics, and today you bring this same fervor to your work on behalf of the American family and your religious values. In doing so, you provide inspiration to a world seeking desperately to find men who can make the message of the Gospel a reality in their lives and times…

"The struggle for freedom in Nicaragua, the effort to defend and strengthen the American family, and, yes, the fight against abortion—all these find a common basis in our belief in a just and loving God, a God who created humankind in His image. 'Without the fostering and defense of these values,' the Holy Father said when I visited him in Rome, 'all human advancement is stunted and the very dignity of the human person is endangered.' The Pope expressed his fervent hope 'that the entire structure of American life will rest ever more securely on the strong foundation of moral and spiritual values.'"

The president profoundly understood what the Order's purpose and mission has been since 1882. He usually closed his addresses to the Knights by emphasizing the two things that have come to shape and define the Order: first prayer, and then action.

"Let us pray that this should come to pass," he said on one occasion. "And let us do what the Knights of Columbus have always been especially good at. Let us work to make it so."

Former President Ronald Reagan speaking at a Knights of Columbus convention, 1982.

CHAPTER FOUR

The 1930s & 1940s

Father Isaias X. Edralin, S.J.

Priests who serve during wartime perform a special kind of service, risking their lives to offer spiritual comfort to the troops. During World War II, few priests were as courageous as Father Isaias Edralin, who endured the Japanese invasion and occupation of the Philippines and still continued to help his people.

Father Isaias Edralin was born on July 5, 1895. Originally a diocesan priest from Nueva Segovia, Father Edralin had a long history with the Knights of Columbus. He became a member of Manila Council 1000, and throughout the 1920s, he helped the Knights to expand, by recruiting candidates for membership wherever he was.

For example, in November 1922, he was serving in Laoag, about 300 miles away from Manila, yet he brought twelve of his parishioners to Manila to join the council there. Meanwhile he worked to organize a center in Laoag, as he did in every city where he served. Father Edralin joined the Jesuits in September of 1933 and became involved in missionary work. In October 1938, just months before World War II broke out, Father Edralin established a unit of Manila Council 1000 in Mindanao. He also served as that group's chaplain. Diego Imperio, past Grand Knight of the unit on Mindanao that would eventually become Cagayan de Oro Council 3108, remembered Father Edralin as "the live wire insofar as Columbianism in Mindanao was concerned. He urged and recruited as many as he could to become Knights of Columbus."

With the war raging, by 1942, many religious personnel had been told to withdraw from certain regions of the Philippines, but Father Edralin was asked by the Bishop to stay on. In late March 1942, Father Edralin was appointed chaplain of the U.S. Army Forces Far East (USAFFE). By May, the Japanese had gained control of much of the country, and Father Edralin, now a member of the U.S. Army, had been taken into custody. After time in a concentration camp, he was placed under house arrest, which allowed him to continue his priestly duties. He counseled everyone who came to him for advice or comfort. He celebrated Mass and made sure that those who died in combat received a proper burial. He offered absolution to those whom he knew were not going to survive, even when this seemed like an impossible challenge. A fellow Jesuit, Father Agustin Consunji, had been arrested and placed in isolation. The Japanese were going to put him to death, and although Father Edralin could not speak with him directly, he managed to catch Father Consunji's attention from a window and raise his right hand to the priest, for the sign of absolution. Father Consunji silently acknowledged the gesture and was soon transferred to Manila, where he was forced to dig his own grave before being executed. The daily job of Father Edralin was to bear witness in the face of the inhumanity of mankind—without losing faith, and without giving in to despair.

After the war, Father Edralin wrote his *Memoirs* and in those pages he described his role with two young Filipino soldiers who'd tried to escape the Japanese concentration camps and were marked for death.

"It was three o'clock in the afternoon," he wrote. "Both boys were prepared spiritually the best I could; they received the sacraments of the Catholic Church and with resignation they accepted their death sentence. The chaplains continued their instruction to the two boys and accompanied them until they were at their graves…The two boys had their hands tied behind their backs. The death march began. The two walked side by side and the two chaplains beside them, whispering prayers and ejaculations before they arrived at a hill outside the barbed wire fence overlooking the quarters where the Japanese commander had his office.

"We marched from the gate to the office of the Japanese commander. From there up towards the hill where some Filipino prisoners had been sent to dig a grave for these two boys…The chaplains…offered the crucifix to be kissed, which the boys did reverently and fervently…The boys were…blindfolded…I then shouted again, 'Jesus, Mary and Joseph. I give you my heart and soul. My Jesus Mercy. My Jesus I love Thee.' After these words, the officer gave me a sign to stop. He commanded the six soldiers to fire and…

"All was over…The following morning I went again to the place of execution to plant the two crosses of the boys, bearing their name, age, rank, town, province and unit and all these carved into the wood so it would not be easily erased. The chaplain planted two branches of trees hoping they grow to mark the place."

Father Edralin was proud of the fact that he never cooperated with the Japanese or gave up any part of his spiritual mission during the war. When he was forced to distribute propaganda leaflets for the occupiers, he made sure that they found their way into the hands of the resistance fighters, so they would know what the Japanese were thinking and planning. In his own way, using the subtle strategies he'd learned from years of wartime service, he fought the enemy with his intelligence and devotion. He was not armed, but he never stopped aiding the Filipinos in their efforts to recapture and reclaim their homeland.

In the late 1940s, Father Edralin was struck with severe arthritis and rheumatism, which forced him into a sickbed in Manila, but his work with the Knights of Columbus bore fruit, when, in February 1948, the unit of Knights he had founded in Cagayan de Oro became Council 3108, the third Council established in the Philippines. The war had taken its toll on Father Edralin, but still, whenever possible, he carried out his priestly duties. He moved to the Culion Leper Colony in Palawan, where he served as superior of the Jesuit chaplaincy. Even in his illness, he continued to serve the Church for three more decades. On the last day of 1974, Father Edralin died of a heart attack in Novaliches.

Through his witnessing and writing, he wanted others to know of the obscure lives that had been cruelly destroyed in the Philippines. He put his heart and soul into his *Memoirs*, in the hope that nothing like World War II would ever happen again. More than half a century later, his words have lost none of their power.

Filipino nuns talk with U.S. soldiers in Manila following the liberation of the Philippines, February 23, 1945.

Father George Willmann, S.J.

He was called the "Father McGivney of the Philippines" because he understood that when men come together with a common faith and a common cause, they can create extraordinary things. Their bond of faith is far more important than their backgrounds or other differences. Born in Brooklyn on June 29, 1897, this Jesuit priest traveled to the Philippines in 1922 while he was still a seminarian to teach at the Ateneo de Manila. He quickly fell in love with the country and its people. He had always hoped to work abroad as a missionary, and now he was anxious to make the Philippines the core of his ministry.

In 1925, he returned to the United States finish his studies in the Jesuit theology program at Woodstock College in Maryland. Upon his return, Willman met with Supreme Knight James A. Flaherty to ask whether a second Knights of Columbus council could be formed in the Philippines. The proposal was not accepted at that time. He returned to the Philippines in 1936, after serving as director of the New York Jesuit Seminary and Mission Bureau, and began to work with the Knights in Manila Council 1000, which he joined in 1938. At that time, it had fewer than 40 members, but he was determined to help it to grow.

By the start of World War II, the Knights had built a presence in the Philippines, even though their numbers remained small. But the war would be devastating to the country as well as to the Knights of Columbus. However, a time of massive tragedy also became a time of great heroism for the Knights. The Philippine Knights organized relief centers—along the lines of the Order's Army Hut program—for servicemen. Father Willmann, who served on the Army-Navy Morale Committee, was one of the leaders of the project. When a boat carrying refugees struck a mine, Father Willmann opened the doors of the Knights of Columbus Hall to the wounded, and helped save nearly 300 lives.

When Manila fell, Father Willmann, being American, was sent to the Santo Tomas concentration camp. But he was able to persuade the commander of the camp to let him continue his priestly and humanitarian ministry. Though occasionally roughed up by Japanese soldiers, Father Willmann was permitted to travel throughout the city to minister to the faithful. After the fall of Corregidor, American and Filipino troops were marched by the Japanese through Manila, right past the Knights of Columbus Hall. Risking death, the Knights rushed outside to give water to the wounded, starving prisoners as they passed.

The example of Father Willmann and his brother Knights of Columbus was so profound that one Catholic Japanese officer sought to join the Knights. Faced with an awkward situation, the Knights were able to turn him down because they were not accepting new members at the time. Father

Willmann later noted that in peacetime the officer, a good Catholic, would have made a great candidate.

Eventually, Father Willmann was held in the Los Baños concentration camp, along with other American missionaries, until its liberation by Allied forces.

During the Japanese occupation, Father Willman repeatedly put himself in danger, but despite being imprisoned and tortured for helping the local population, he never wavered. His bravery and dedication to the Filipinos in the worst of times laid the groundwork for what would happen in the better days ahead. After the war, the Knights under Father Willmann's leadership opened several clubs for allied soldiers—many of whom were coming out of Japanese concentration camps. There the men had their health restored in these Catholic-led facilities, which received much of their funding from the Knights of Columbus in the United States.

In 1947, Father Willmann was still stationed in the Philippines when he visited the United States and persuaded Supreme Knight Luke E. Hart that the moment had come to expand the Order in the Pacific. Father Willmann wanted to institute three Filipino councils and was relentless in promoting this idea. Hart was soon convinced of the soundness of this plan, confident that no one had a better feel for the needs and aspirations of the Filipinos than Father Willmann. In October 1947, the Board approved the proposal and the timing was perfect. In the aftermath of the war's destruction, Filipino Catholic men were looking for ways to rebuild their lives, spiritually and physically. When the Supreme Knight visited the Philippines in 1955, he found more than 50 vibrant councils operating in the islands.

Within two decades, Father Willmann had compiled a stunning record of achievement in the Philippines. In 1938, he had established the Catholic Youth Organization at the University of the Philippines, where he served as chaplain from 1938–40. In 1946, he founded a Catholic press, publishing *Filipinas* and *Cross* magazines. In 1950, he brought the Columbian Squires to the Philippines and the next year he organized the Daughters of Isabella and the Columbian Farmers Aid Association, which later evolved into the Knights of Columbus Community Service, Inc. Then came the Knights of Columbus Fraternal Association of the Philippines, which offered life insurance to members there for the first time, and the Knights of Columbus Philippines Foundation, Inc., which provides educational benefits to poor students, and funds relief efforts after natural disasters.

Father Willmann was the Philippines' first District Deputy and in 1954 he was appointed Territorial Deputy, a position he held until 1977. In 1975, he was given Philippine citizenship, and in 1977, his work was honored by the pope. Also that year, he came to America to attend the Ninety-Fifth Annual Supreme Convention in Indianapolis. Following the convention, he traveled to New York City to visit his sister, Ruth, a Franciscan nun. In New York, the 80-year-old priest suffered a fall and broke his hip. While recovering from surgery that had apparently been successful, he went into cardiac arrest and died, on September 14, 1977. The news of his death shook the entire Catholic community in the Philippines. The man who'd struggled alongside them in World War II and brought the Order into their lives throughout the post-war era was suddenly gone. But his legacy was firmly in place in Manila and throughout the islands, and the greatest days of expansion lay ahead.

When Fr. Willmann joined the Knights of Columbus in the Philippines in 1938, there was one council with about 35 active members. When he died 39 years later, there were 457 councils and 29,408 members. The "Father McGivney of the Philippines" will always be remembered fondly by the people of his adopted land.

Father George Willmann (left) at a Knights of Columbus event in the Philippines.

Myles E. Connolly

Myles Connolly was born in Boston on October 7, 1897. After graduating from Boston College in 1918, he began his career as a feature writer for the *Boston Post*. Then, in 1924 he went to New Haven to be the editor of *Columbia*, the official periodical of the Knights of Columbus. During the next four years, Myles Connolly edited everything that appeared in its pages and wrote three-quarters of the magazine himself—in the middle of the night. The daytime, he firmly believed, was for sleeping and the dark hours for working, talking with friends or playing bridge. Every day he arose in mid-afternoon and ate breakfast at 4 P.M. He arrived at the *Columbia* office an hour later, worked until 10 P.M., went out for lunch, came back and finished up around 4 A.M. He ate dinner at a Childs all-night restaurant and headed home. By dawn, he would be ready for bed, unless he got into a card game or was deeply involved in a new piece of writing. In the small hours before dawn, he unwound, lit up a cigar, let his imagination run free, and put together his first book, a humorous 1928 novel called *Mr. Blue*. It was about an idealistic young man who gave away a fortune as he applied Christian teachings to everyday life. The narrator of the story is a businessman who doesn't quite know what to make of Blue's faith and idealism. The book became a bestseller, and was reissued four times, introducing new generations to the young man who was opposed to materialism and decided to do something about it.

While still working at *Columbia*, Connolly turned out both fiction and nonfiction, learning the trade of screen-writing that he would carry into the world and display to an audience of millions in Hollywood. It was Joseph P. Kennedy who, because he was impressed with Connolly's writing, suggested that he try his luck in the movies. Despite the enormous success he would find after leaving New Haven for Los Angeles, Connolly never moved far away from the roots and convictions he employed as *Columbia*'s editor. From the beginning, whether writing for the Knights of Columbus or for movie stars, he devoted himself to what he fervently called "Catholic writing," a term that carried a special meaning for him.

He described it this way in a Catholic newspaper called *The Pilot*: "Mentioning Our Lord or Our Lady does not mean you're an artist…To me, a book is Catholic if it tells in concrete terms man's relation to his God and to his soul. Why can't some of our writers talk more about the adventure of Catholicism?"

Connolly spent his life describing that adventure. After leaving *Columbia*, he wrote short stories, novels, and a series of blockbuster movie scripts, always leaning toward comedy because he felt that anyone could write about "how futile, how evil, everything is in this modern day and age…But to write comedy…you have to lift your head high up into the clear, fresh air so that you can catch the wonderful, tinkling sound of laughter."

His books were popular but he was best known for his screenplays, which touched virtually everyone who came in contact with popular culture in the 1930s and '40s. He wrote or cowrote *Mr. Smith Goes to Washington*, starring James Stewart and Jean Arthur; *Mr. Deeds Goes to Town* and *Meet John Doe*, both featuring Gary Cooper; *State of the Union*, with Spencer Tracy and Katharine Hepburn; and *My Son John*, starring Helen Hayes—plus several Tarzan movies and a number of high-budget MGM musicals. He smoked a lot of cigars and saw a lot of dawns while bringing to life a series of fictional American heroes.

In whatever he wrote, he sought to create not just wholesome stories with good characters—people who could teach the viewers something about making the right decisions in life—but aimed for something more. He believed that the real journey for every man and woman was the one taken with God, so he put his protagonists into dramatic, difficult situations and had them choose the way that served not just their own selfish interests, but something beyond that narrow path. He made certain that their decisions were spiritually grounded and socially important. The closer his people came to making sacrifices and helping others, the closer they stood to God. This was what he'd learned from the Church and through his long association with the Knights of Columbus, and to Connolly, this was the true "Catholic adventure."

It wasn't enough, he believed, to be an entertaining writer. It was also necessary to educate, in the deepest sense of the word, by showing that choices had consequences, and that good choices always had the capacity to change life for the better. He not only found a wide audience but achieved one of the greatest things a writer can hope for: without being at all pedantic or preachy, he found a way to channel his core convictions into popular stories that moved countless people. The movie scripts he wrote are still seen on television, and both his humor and his message can be experienced by anyone who watches his films or reads his books. Although he died in July of 1964, Myles Connolly's "Catholic adventures" still remain a rich part of our cultural heritage.

A scene from Mr. Smith Goes to Town, *written by Myles Connolly and starring James Stewart, 1939.*

Oscar Ledesma

He was an unassuming Filipino who went to work early in the morning and stayed in the office till late at night. He took care of the details without ever losing sight of the larger vision he was serving. During his long career as a lawyer, an ambassador, and a Knights of Columbus official, he mingled with presidents and other dignitaries from around the world, while never letting this affect his attitude or his behavior toward less fortunate people. He was completely worthy and completely qualified for the role he would one day play for his nation.

It fell to Oscar Ledesma to follow in the footsteps of Jesuit Father George Willmann, the pioneer who brought the Knights of Columbus to the Philippines during the first half of the 20th century. Willmann was known as the "Father McGivney of the Philippines," while Ledesma was the perfect successor, consolidating the position of the Knights in the Pacific and steadily growing the membership of the Order in the islands. The two men together—first Father Willmann and then Oscar Ledesma—made certain that the Knights would flourish in the Philippines and they gave the Order a truly international flavor.

Oscar was born in Silay, Negros Occidental, Visayas, in 1902 and 23 years later earned his law degree at the University of the Philippines. He worked as an attorney before entering the political realm as the Mayor of Iloilo and then, in 1942, as Governor. From 1954–57, he was the Philippine Secretary of Commerce and in 1963 he became that country's Ambassador to the United States. He traveled around the globe, meeting leaders from the Far East, the Soviet Union, and Australia, but he was also a family man, fathering nine children and raising them with his wife, Juanita. By the mid-'70s, he'd fulfilled most of his professional ambitions, but retirement was not in his plans.

In September 1977, Father Willmann died in New York City from complications after falling and breaking his hip. The Knights in the Philippines were suddenly without a Territorial Deputy. Supreme Knight Virgil Dechant was keenly aware of Ledesma's contributions to both his country and to the Order, so he quickly appointed Ledesma as the new Territorial Deputy. Ledesma had the experience to make such a decision easy. Prior to his appointment, he had served as Assistant Deputy for Luzon and Western Visayas, President of the Knights of Columbus Community Services, Inc. (KCCSI), Trustee of the Knights of Columbus Fraternal Association of the Philippines, Inc. (KCFAPI), and President of the Knights of Columbus Foundation of the Philippines. He had also served the church as president of Catholic action, and as an active participant in Friends of the Lepers, and several other charitable organizations.

Ledesma's first official message to the Knights was to carry out the last appeal of Father Willmann: "to spiritualize all of our activities, for whatever we do as Knights of Columbus must be related to our Faith, and must be Christ-oriented." Ledesma wanted Filipino men to not express their spirituality only when attending Mass or a Knights of Columbus meeting, but to infuse their daily routines—their interactions with families and friends or on the job—with the same reverence and love that they brought to a sacramental ceremony. Being a Knight meant serving a larger set of goals both in public and in private matters.

Ledesma ran the Order with the same efficiency as Father Willmann, and under his leadership it expanded significantly. When he took over as Philippines Deputy in 1978, there were 29,408 Knights in 457 Councils in that country. When he left the post six years later, there were 53,213 Knights in 696 Councils—a leap of 80%. His gentle, steady example of leadership inspired others to recruit for the Order, but as Philippines Deputy, he also revealed a very practical side. His business acumen was crucial in bringing a Knights of Columbus life insurance program to Filipino members and their families through the Knights of Columbus Fraternal Association of the Philippines. (Now known as the "KC Fraternal," the program was established in 1958.)

Ledesma's accomplishments won him many honors. Pope Paul VI conferred upon him the rank of Knight Commander in the Order of Pope Saint Sylvester. In 1983, the Knights named him an Honorary Member of the Board of Directors and eight years later he was designated as Supreme Director Emeritus. Supreme Knight Virgil Dechant visited Ledesma in the Philippines and the excursion made a lasting impression on him.

"During that lengthy trip," the Supreme Knight wrote, "it was obvious to me how greatly Don Oscar and Dona Juana were loved and appreciated by the thousands of Knights and families we met. Not only that—when we were tempted to yield to the tiredness caused by the rigors of the journey, we only had to look at the Ledesmas to be revivified with renewed energy and enthusiasm."

It was also obvious that Don Oscar had never stopped building on his predecessor's great legacy in the Philippines. He remained Supreme Director Emeritus until his death in 1993, following Father Willmann's charge to spiritualize every moment of his life to the very end.

Oscar Ledesma (second from right) meets with Father George Willmann (first from left) and two members of the Knights of Columbus.

Ernest I. King

King was known for his sense of humor, and it was something he often used in dealing with the tensions of living in a segregated society. He carried in his memory countless jokes, with just the right story for any occasion. He refused to give in to bitterness when confronted with racism because he knew that to follow Christ was to choose love and forgiveness over anger and hatred. Humor was a good way of overcoming the divisions in society, and organizing was another. In 1946, he was a leader in creating the North Carolina Catholic Laymen's Association, an interracial group formed to foster better relations between blacks and whites. He served on the organization's board of directors and as its chairman. He knew that during the 19th century, St. Thomas the Apostle Church had served all of Wilmington's Catholics, both black and white, and worked hard for the day when it would do so once again.

In 1951, he started a youth group at St. Thomas, and four years later Bishop Vincent S. Waters designated him as the Outstanding Youth Leader in the Raleigh Diocese, then covering the entire state of North Carolina. In 1961, he joined the Knights of Columbus and in 1966 he became a Grand Knight. Two years after that, he was named District Deputy and then won election as State Deputy, only the fourth African American to reach this level and the first who lived below the Mason-Dixon line. Along the way, he was the publisher-editor of the *Tar Heel Knight*, the periodical of the North Carolina Knights of Columbus. By the mid 1970s, in large part because of the work of men like Ernest King, St. Thomas the Apostle was fully integrated. And when the church merged with St. Mary's in the 1960s, he became the authority on its history. His light touch, which was evident in most every speech he ever made for the Order, was highly successful at disarming people and bringing blacks and white together. He could tell an hour's worth of jokes without pausing, and all were suitable for the whole family.

King was as innovative in his working life as he was in his efforts on behalf of racial harmony and the Catholic faith.

Born on October 26, 1901, in Wilmington, North Carolina, Ernest King was raised a Baptist but wasn't really sure that was the church where he belonged. At sixteen he encountered Catholicism and ultimately decided to convert. He joined the oldest Catholic church in North Carolina, St. Thomas the Apostle parish in Wilmington. It was the first step on a journey that eventually led him to the Knights of Columbus, and to becoming the first African American from the South to hold the post of State Deputy, a position in which he would serve two terms.

He earned a living in a remarkable variety of ways. For a time, he made wooden picture frames, and then he strung tennis rackets. For half a decade he was butler to a career diplomat in Wilmington named Fred Morris Dearing. King became the maitre d' of an exclusive local nightclub called the Plantation Club and later he taught cooking at Wilmington High School. For many years he also catered banquets for the Order and other organizations.

It was the sense of camaraderie with other Catholic men and the charity work that originally drew him to the Knights of Columbus. After becoming a member and later an officer, he was determined to help carry on that tradition of giving. As State Deputy in North Carolina, he oversaw a major project to raise money for the mentally disabled. Called "Operation Lamb," it brought in $2,000 in its inaugural year of 1974, $57,000 in 1975, and more than $76,000 in 1976.

King always credited the Knights with making far more of his life than he could have made of it without them. You've got to believe in something bigger than yourself, he told everyone who asked him about the benefits of being in the Order, or you will never realize your potential. He not only fulfilled his own potential but did so with humor and grace. When he died in July 1983, the newspapers reported that he was "possibly one of the best known black Catholics in the country." Ernest King lived a life filled with faith and love, and gave the gift of laughter to everyone he met.

Ernest King and other Knights during a Mass held at the Supreme Convention in Boston, Massachusetts, August 17, 1976.

Father William P. Ryan

William Patrick Ryan simply knew it at an early age. One day when he was in the fifth grade, he walked out of the front door of his school and stared for a moment at South Boston's Gate of Heaven Catholic Church across the street. As his eyes focused on the cross atop the steeple, Ryan knew with certainty he would be a priest. What he did not know at the time was that his vocation would ultimately put him at the heart of the great civil rights struggle of the 20th century.

Ryan was born to Irish Catholic immigrant parents in 1910 in Morris, Connecticut. During his formative years, he was heavily influenced by his father's powerful commitment to social justice; he would adopt that commitment and make it the centerpiece of his ministry for the rest of his life.

After graduating from Boston College in 1932 he entered St. John Seminary in Boston, planning to become a diocesan priest. But in a twist of fate, Boston's Cardinal Archbishop William O'Connell decided he had plenty of priests and too many seminarians, and ordered that half the seminarians at St. John's be dropped. Ryan was one of them. Undaunted, he then turned to a Catholic order called the Oblates of Mary Immaculate, which was happy to have him. William Ryan was ordained in June 1938, at the National Shrine of the Immaculate Conception in Washington, D.C.

Father Ryan's first assignment as a priest was in Fayetteville, North Carolina, where he was sent to minister to the city's small African American Catholic community. It was the beginning of a ministry that would be far different than the one he'd anticipated when he entered St. John's. Massachusetts and North Carolina were worlds apart. There was already a Catholic church in Fayetteville, but in the 1930s the South was thoroughly segregated. And so Father Ryan's first Masses were held in a local barbershop. The congregation was very poor, and the first collection totaled 75 cents.

Because he couldn't use the existing Catholic church where white parishioners went, he developed plans to build a church for his black congregation. The project would require raising $16,000, no small challenge for a parish as poor as his. Father Ryan traveled back to Boston to raise funds for the project, and stopped in to see Monseigner (later Cardinal) Richard Cushing, who was then at the Society for the Propagation of the Faith. Monseigner Cushing said that a donation of $4,500 had been made in honor of a deceased priest, and offered it to Father Ryan on one condition: that he'd name his new church St. Ann's, after the parish in Boston that had raised the money. He readily agreed.

Father Ryan served as pastor of St. Ann's church in Fayetteville for more than a dozen years, and during the 1940s substantial numbers of African Americans became Roman Catholic. His parish grew steadily, and in 1941 he became active in Cardinal Gibbons Council 2838. But he was outraged by the racial segregation that his people had to endure, and was sharply critical of segregation generally, as well as within the Catholic community. By 1951, tensions were high, and Father Ryan's outspoken criticism of segregation brought death threats against him. The bishop of Raleigh-Durham took the threats very seriously, and pulled Father Ryan out of Fayetteville to ensure that he would not become the victim of murder. He was transferred to Indiana, where he served as pastor of a church in Indianapolis until 1962. Throughout the turbulent 1950s and '60s, Father Ryan was active in the Civil Rights movement, and he sometimes marched with the Reverend Martin Luther King.

In 1962, Father. Ryan was elected Provincial for the Eastern Province of the Oblates of Mary Immaculate, a position he held for six years. As Provincial he traveled extensively and met two popes, John XXIII and Paul VI. In 1968 he returned to St. Ann's Church in Fayetteville and served there until his health deteriorated in 1971. Times were changing in North Carolina. The racism Father Ryan had

fought so hard against was finally beginning to fade. The Civil Rights legislation of the 1960s had become an established part of American law, and real progress had flowed from this. One man who'd been a part of the group that had wanted to kill Father Ryan back in 1951 came forward and confessed his involvement in the plot. Far from turning his back on this individual, Father Ryan embraced him as someone willing to look at himself truthfully, admit wrongdoing, and set things right. The two men were reconciled and it was one more heartfelt victory in a life filled with such triumphs.

After 55 years as a priest, Father Ryan died on Christmas Eve 1993. But his legacy would stretch far into the future. In 1995, the men of St. Ann's formed the Reverend William P. Ryan Council 11683, and most of the Knights in the new council were African American. Father Ryan's nephew, Deacon Kenneth Ryan, Supreme Treasurer of the Knights of Columbus, voted as Supreme Director to ratify the charter for the new council. Two weeks before his death, Father Ryan had given his nephew his Fourth Degree lapel pin, knowing his nephew would carry on his work.

Although less well known than Martin Luther King, Father William Ryan made a significant contribution to the battle for civil rights for every American, and he did so with courage, love, and deep faith.

Father William Ryan during his audience with Pope Paul VI.

CHAPTER FIVE

The 1950s & 1960s

Jorge J. Hyatt

Throughout the history of the Knights of Columbus, members have found themselves involved in some of the most momentous events of their times. From the wars of the 20th century to the terrorist attacks of September 11, 2001, Knights have been witnesses to and participants in many of the most harrowing and difficult moments in modern history. This is particularly true in places where freedom—especially religious freedom—has been under siege. In the 1920s, when Mexico's government violently suppressed the Catholic church, Knights and priests fiercely defended their faith and some paid with their lives. When Japanese forces cruelly occupied the Philippines during World War II, Knights provided support to captured American and Filipino soldiers and civilians who were hauled off to internment camps.

The Cuban Revolution was another example. In 1959, Fidel Castro and his forces seized power in Cuba, and within a few years a brutal crackdown on religious freedoms of the overwhelmingly Catholic (85 percent) population was underway. In 1962 Cuba became an officially atheist state, and the Castro regime proceeded to seize and shut down more than 400 Catholic schools. Tens of thousands of Cubans never accepted his rule and almost immediately began using any possible means to escape his dictatorship. Naturally, they turned their attention ninety miles north, to the United States and Miami, Florida. Ever since the late '50s, a steady stream of Cubans has fled the Castro regime and reestablished working lives, family lives, and religious lives in America. The Order has played an integral role in that process.

Jorge Hyatt was part of the wave of Cubans who managed to escape during the first year or so after Castro's revolution. Born in 1902, he had been a Knight of Columbus for many years, having joined San Augustin Council 1390 in Havana in 1923. He had served as Financial Secretary from 1932–1941 and again from 1946-61, and as Grand Knight from 1942–45. He joined because he saw the Knights "as an ideal body of Catholic men, capable and free by its very own character to defend the rights and dignity of the Church of Catholics as citizens in all aspects of life."

Throughout the first half of the twentieth century, Cuba—like much of Latin America—suffered a great deal of political turmoil. Governments changed often and there was a strong anti-clerical sentiment in the country because the Church was identified with Spain, the former colonial master. "Religion seemed to be limited to women," Hyatt once explained. He was able to be an active Catholic in Cuba through the Knights of Columbus, however, because the Knights were not identified with Spain and were regarded as sufficiently independent of the Catholic hierarchy. As president of the Catholic University Student Club in Havana and a member of the Knights of Columbus, he and his council were able to successfully block a resolution at the university students' convention that would have condemned Catholic education in schools.

With the coming of the Cuban revolution, he made plans to leave his homeland and by 1961, he had temporarily relocated to Rolla, Missouri, to be near his son, who was studying engineering at the University of Missouri. From there, he wrote to Supreme Knight Luke Hart and told him that he feared going back to Cuba because he knew he would be arrested and permanently detained. If he stayed in America, would the Order help him find employment? His first choice was to work as a translator or to assist other Cuban refugees looking for work. The Supreme Knight assured Hyatt that he would do what he could, and thanks to the efforts of the Knights, he was able to remain in the United States.

On January 8, 1961, Luis Felipe Lay and Florida State Deputy John Adamson started a council in Miami for Cuban refugees. At the time, the founders believed that the Cuban revolution would be short-lived and the refugees would soon be able to return to the island. The council, Our Lady of Charity 5110, was bolstered when the Supreme Council sent it $10,000 for a relief fund for Cuban members and their dependents. A reception center was created to provide help for the growing refugee population until the U.S. government could offer more assistance. By 1962, Knights from across the nation were sending money to Miami to aid the refugees. The initial financial support these people received in America came from the Order.

It played a vital role in obtaining visa waivers for the refugees entering America. The Knights would get an endorsement for a refugee from an elected representative, and then forward it to the State Department. No accurate data exist to document the number of Cubans for whom this effort meant safe refuge on Florida's shores, but one thing is certain: those who came to America were forever grateful for the help they received in a time of crisis. Having fled Castro's dictatorship, they never went back to Cuba. Instead, they found work, had families, and put down roots in their new homeland. And being overwhelmingly Catholic, many became Knights in the United States, if they hadn't already been members back in their homeland.

Ultimately, Jorge Hyatt too found a new home in America. He settled in New Haven, Connecticut, where the Knights of Columbus headquarters was located. He was hired to work as a translator and consultant to Cuban refugees, a position he held from 1961 until his death on April 25, 1990, at the age of 88. He assisted countless families in rebuilding their lives in the United States and reestablishing their connection to the Church. What they could no longer find in Cuba, they began creating with Hyatt's help in the Unite States.

After more than three decades in power, Castro began to soften—ever so slightly—his regime's stance on religion. In 1992, the Cuban constitution changed the government's posture from "atheist" to "secular." And in January of 1998, nearly eight years after Jorge Hyatt's death, Pope John Paul II was allowed to make an official visit to Cuba. When John Paul died in April 2005, Fidel Castro personally attended a memorial Mass at the Catholic cathedral in Havana, and signed the condolence book. Today, there are still believed to be Knights of Columbus in Cuba, although they're not allowed to meet or function as an organization. Led by Cardinal Archbishop Jaime L. Ortega, Catholics in Cuba are able to worship, but still may not operate schools or openly oppose the government's policies. The spiritual descendants of Jorge Hyatt on both sides of the Florida straits continue to pray for the day when Cuba will once again be free, and when Hyatt's beloved Knights will again be able to serve as the strong right arm of the Catholic church in Cuba.

Jorge Hyatt (tenth from left) is present at a ceremony where gifts from Havana, Cuba, are presented to Cuban refugees.

John Fitzgerald Kennedy

As much as Al Smith, the first major party Catholic candidate to run for president, was the product of his impoverished background, John Fitzgerald Kennedy was the product of an Irish-American Catholic family that became very prosperous. His father, Joseph P. Kennedy, had watched Smith campaign for the Oval Office in 1928

and get crushed, not just by his opponent, Herbert Hoover, but by a virulent anti-Catholic sentiment in American politics. Right then, Joe Kennedy committed himself not merely to electing a Catholic president in his lifetime, but to ensuring that the first Catholic president would be one of his own sons. Joe had hoped to see his namesake, the younger Joseph Kennedy, win the White House, but Joe Jr. died in Europe during World War II. John, who learned of his brother's death while he was in a Navy hospital recovering from his own war injuries, was next in line.

Where Al Smith came from a working class background and never finished high school, JFK had the advantage of being both upper class and Harvard-educated. Despite that, more than three decades after Smith had begun to clear the path for a Catholic president, Kennedy still had to face what remained of anti-Catholic prejudice in America. By 1960, there had been literally thousands of very successful Catholic politicians all over the country, but JFK would not settle for being a governor or senator, and resolved to take the last step for Catholics everywhere by becoming the president of the United States. Like Smith, Kennedy brought to the race two important traits: a strong Catholic upbringing and the values and spirit of the Knights of Columbus (he was a member of Bunker Hill Council 62 in Charlestown, Massachusetts).

Overcoming the last vestiges of anti-Catholic prejudice in 1960 was no easy matter, and not every Catholic was happy with his assurances to a group of Protestant ministers in Houston that they need not fear having him as president: "I am not the Catholic candidate for President," he said. "I am the Democratic Party's candidate for President who happens also to be a Catholic. I do not speak for my church on public matters, and the church does not speak for me."

But those widely reported remarks were followed later in the speech by a ringing condemnation of anti-Catholic prejudice. He would not apologize for his views on the subject, "nor do I intend to disavow either my views or my church in order to win this election. If I should lose on the real issues, I shall return to my seat in the Senate, satisfied that I'd tried my best and was fairly judged. But if this election is decided on the basis that 40 million Americans lost their chance of being President on the day they were baptized, then it is the whole nation that will be the loser, in the eyes of Catholics and non-Catholics around the world, in the eyes of history, and in the eyes of our own people." The clarity and simple justice of his appeal to the better side of the American people carried the day, although his winning margin was paper-thin.

He ran for office on the notion that it was time for a new generation to take the helm in America, and that a new frontier was ready to be explored. Catholics embraced the man and the message. He received 78% of the Catholic vote in 1960 and that made the difference in his narrow victory. If his triumph was a win for every Catholic, nowhere was that truer than among his fellow Knights, who'd been insisting on their ability to be both faithful Catholics and patriotic Americans since the 19th century.

John Kennedy was born on May 29, 1917, one of nine children that his mother, Rose, and father, Joe, would have. Jack (as he was called) was not a healthy baby and he battled scarlet fever when he was three. Throughout his life, he

The marriage ceremony of John F. Kennedy and Jacqueline Bouvier, September 12, 1953.

Exemplification of the Fourth Degree, Fall River, Massachusetts, May 30, 1954. Left to right: Faithful Navigator Charles F. Williams, Jr., Bishop Connelly, Master John McDevitt, and U.S. Senator John F. Kennedy.

would have a number of health problems, but he never let them slow him down. He graduated from Harvard in 1940, after which he entered the Navy, and he served in the South Pacific during World War II. In 1943, he was the commander of PT 109, a patrol torpedo boat that was sunk by a Japanese destroyer; despite his own injuries, he saved the life of one of his men and was later awarded the Navy and Marine Corps Medal for bravery. Jack was welcomed into the Knights of Columbus on St. Patrick's Day in 1946, months after his release from the Navy at the end of the war. On his Knights of Columbus membership application, Kennedy noted that his present occupation was "correspondent" (he was working as a reporter for the Hearst newspapers), and in the box that asked, "Do you intend changing your present occupation?" he wrote, "not sure." Not too many weeks later, however, he became a candidate for the U.S. House of Representatives, and he won easily in the fall of 1946. Reelected in 1948 and 1950, he moved up to the U.S. Senate in 1952. In 1953, he and Jacqueline Bouvier, a Washington, D.C., journalist, were married by Boston's Richard Cardinal Cushing, who remained a close friend of the Kennedy family over the years. In 1954, Jack became a Fourth Degree Knight in a ceremony presided over by John McDevitt, who would later become Supreme Knight while Kennedy was president.

John Kennedy's youthful appeal (at 44, he became the youngest man ever elected president) and idealism set the tone for a post-war generation then coming to maturity. His book *Profiles in Courage*, written while he was recovering from back surgery in 1955, won the Pulitzer Prize. His clarion call to public service as he began his presidency would go down in history as one of the most memorable and inspiring speeches by any American political leader.

"Ask not," he said during his inaugural speech on a cold day in January 1961, "what your country can do for you, ask what you can do for your country."

With the help of fellow Knight Sargent Shriver (see page 94), Kennedy would soon offer Americans who shared his idealism an opportunity to serve people in need through the Peace Corps and a variety of domestic programs. He also had to face the challenge of an America that was changing: in 1954, segregation had been outlawed, but racism persisted. The civil rights movement was well underway during his presidency, and he spoke out on behalf of the need for a new civil rights bill. Many in the leadership of the Knights were strongly supportive of civil rights, including John McDevitt (see page 76). Throughout his presidency, he regarded his relationship with his brother Knights as especially important. "President Kennedy told me to make sure that his membership in the Knights of Columbus did not lapse," his personal

John F. Kennedy meeting with Supreme Knight Luke Hart.

secretary, Evelyn Lincoln said later. "He also told me to make sure that I made up a check for his signature each time that a dues notice would arrive." He welcomed Supreme Knight Luke Hart into the Oval Office, where he received a framed copy of the Pledge of Allegiance. In November 1963, Kennedy's assassination in Dallas shocked the nation and the world. The horrible event "brought to us and to all the world grief so profound and so personal that it will not soon subside," the Knights of Columbus Board of Directors declared. "However heavily he was occupied with the demands of his high office, there poured out of him a sympathy and concern for the least of his fellow men so genuine and so spontaneous that his death brought, throughout the world, tears that are shed only for the loss of a friend.

"Taken from us in the fullness of his life, President John Fitzgerald Kennedy has left with us, and with the multitudes everywhere who were inspired by his courage and heartened by his optimism and charity, a living example of a man who, in his own words, stated the rule by which he lived and to which he was faithful to the end. Greater love hath no man."

Today, 29 Knights of Columbus councils are named after John F. Kennedy, "this Brother Knight and great American who lives on in the affectionate memory of millions who placed in him their trust and their hope for peace and freedom."

John F. Kennedy on the cover of Time *magazine, November 14, 1983.*

Vincent T. Lombardi

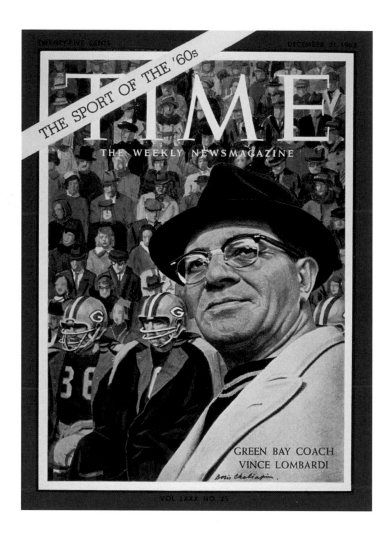

THE SPORT OF THE '60s

TIME

THE WEEKLY NEWSMAGAZINE

GREEN BAY COACH
VINCE LOMBARDI

Who was Vince Lombardi? The world knew him as the spectacularly successful coach of the Green Bay Packers who once said, "Winning isn't everything—it's the only thing," but there was far more to Lombardi than that. Born on June 11, 1913, he was the son of a butcher, one of five children of Henry and Matilda Lombardi of Brooklyn, New York. And while Vince was known for being a tough-talking football coach, before there was coaching, he had spent two years in a seminary studying for the priesthood; he played football at Fordham University on a defensive line known as the "Seven Blocks of Granite," and studied law in Fordham's night school.

He also taught Latin, algebra, and physics at St. Cecilia's, a Catholic high school in New Jersey, before becoming a coach at West Point and then taking a job as assistant coach with the New York Giants of the National Football League. His achievements in the NFL would inspire tens of millions, as he himself was inspired by his formation as a Catholic and his life as a Knight. He never wanted the easy assignments in football or elsewhere, but sought out the biggest challenges he could find.

For years Green Bay, Wisconsin, was barely able to sustain its hometown-owned pro football team. The Packers had been named for the local meatpacking industry and little Green Bay (population 98,000) had to compete with the likes of the New York Giants, the Chicago Bears, and the Washington Redskins. By the late 1950s, all three of these teams had produced legendary players or coaches, while Green Bay had struggled just to survive. In 1958, the Pack's record was one win, ten losses, and a tie. They'd hit bottom and badly needed an infusion of football intelligence and fire. They took a chance by hiring a tough-faced, gravel-voiced coach who'd never led an NFL team. To Lombardi this meant only one thing: he had a lot to prove and not much time to prove it.

Very quickly, he took charge of the faltering franchise, determined to turn it around. He tightened up discipline and simplified the game. The Packers were going to block hard and tackle hard and hit people all over the field, and if they didn't want to do that, he'd find other players. If they were willing to follow his vision, he promised them success. Lombardi was one of those men who knew exactly what he wanted on the gridiron all the time—perfection. It was just that simple.

"If you believe in yourself," he said, "and have the courage, the determination, the dedication, the competitive drive, and if you are willing to sacrifice the little things in life and pay the price for the things that are worthwhile, it can be done. Once a man has made a commitment to a way of life, he puts the greatest strength in the world behind him. It's something we call heart power. Once a man has made this commitment, nothing will stop him short of success."

His first year with the Pack, the team went 7–5. This record wasn't all he hoped for, but the corner had been turned and the message had been sent to his players and the rest of the league. Green Bay had a new coach and a new attitude.

Football men are known for being very driven and maybe just a little bit crazy. Who else would dare try to get 11 big athletes to perform in total unison during every moment of every game? Who else takes each mistake an employee makes so personally that it causes his temper to rise and makes him constantly pace the sidelines, shouting out instructions or shouting at the referees? Lombardi the coach wasn't known for his timid manner and quiet words. He demanded respect from every player and he got it, but off the field, he was a much different man, with just as strong a commitment to ethics and justice. A Fourth Degree Knight of Columbus, he served on the Green Bay City Council for Human Relations and the Citizens Committee of St. Norbert College. He was Green Bay's chairman of the Cancer Fund and president of the Wisconsin Mental Health Association. On road trips with the Packers, he regularly led the Catholic players to Mass. He expected them to give as much commit- ment to their faith as they gave to their work on the gridiron.

With his grounding in hard work and sacrifice, and with his exacting plan for what a football team should do, all he needed were the right players. In the early '60s, he picked up a great field leader in quarterback Bart Starr, as quiet as Lombardi was demonstrative, and then he found two stellar running backs: the speedy Paul Hornung and the steam- rolling Jim Taylor. He put together a group of good receivers, led by Max McGee, and the toughest defense the league had yet seen, headed by Herb Adderly and Ray Nitschke. Now it was up to the head coach to prod, poke, inspire, and motivate the Packers to reach their potential. Lombardi was a master at using a sort of "tough love"; players feared him, but they also respected him and didn't want to let him down. Through his coaching, they learned to play better than they ever thought they could, and the team began to perform at the level the coach expected. In 1961, the Packers defeated the New York Giants to become world champions. They repeated in 1962. Three years later, they won the title again, making Green Bay the official home of a football dynasty. The franchise was now thriving and able to expand its stadium by 8,000 seats to more than 50,000.

Back in those days, before the NFL had become America's most popular sport, it needed a mythic figure pacing the sidelines, someone the TV cameras could focus on to show fans how a real pro football coach looked and behaved. It needed somebody capable of molding a group of athletes into an unstoppable force—and Lombardi filled that role perfectly. While the rest of 1960s society was growing more lax and laid-back about many things, Lombardi continued to believe that problems could be solved through hard work, self-discipline, and faith. He did not believe in shortcuts or excuses. He set a positive example, and his players followed him, not because they always liked him, but because he was a natural-born leader and his system produced excellence.

When the '60s ended, he left the Pack, and they were never the same without him. He died of cancer in September 1970, and thousands attended his funeral. Several Knights of Columbus chapters were named after him, including Council 6522 in Middletown, New Jersey. And to this day, he is still mentioned as proof that good coaching can create champi- onship teams. That's why the award the winning Super Bowl team gets each year is called the Lombardi Trophy.

Vince Lombardi and his team celebrate a win for the Green Bay Packers.

Major General Patrick H. Brady

Pat Brady served with distinction for 34 years in the U.S. military but is primarily known his actions during one day. On January 6, 1968, battles were raging throughout South Vietnam and casualties were everywhere. Several helicopter pilots had attempted to rescue wounded American and South Vietnamese soldiers from a battlefield in enemy-held territory, but all had failed because conditions were too tough. With men dying because they couldn't be reached in the field, the U.S. command asked for a volunteer to fly into combat and save those who could be saved. When other pilots answered with silence, Major Brady stepped forward and took the controls of a UH-1H ambulance helicopter near Chu Lai. As a member of the Army's 44th Medical

Brigade, he'd flown many dangerous missions, but never one like this. More than courage was needed because he spontaneously had to invent tactical and foul-weather flying techniques never before tried under fire.

The first location he flew into was heavily defended by Viet Cong and covered by dense fog. Dropping the chopper down through smoke and mist, Major Brady hovered over a small trail, turning the craft sideward so its blades created a backwash that blew away the fog and give him a landing target. As he descended farther, the fog parted but that generated more trouble. The enemy could now clearly see him and unleashed round after round at his craft. The chopper took some hits, but not enough to bring it down or turn away Major Brady. The landing site was dangerously small, but gingerly he lowered the helicopter and picked up two badly hurt South Vietnamese soldiers, departing the area with only minor damage to the UH-1H.

After delivering the soldiers to safety, he flew to another site completely shrouded by fog, where a pair of American choppers had already been shot down and casualties lay only 50 meters from the Viet Cong. Using the same skills he'd employed earlier in the day—and exceptional courage—Major Brady made four separate flights into this combat zone and each time he brought out more wounded. On the third leg, he dropped into an area completely surrounded by the enemy. In order to reach the landing zone and make a rescue, the Major had to land on a pinpoint target, not once but twice. His helicopter had been hit repeatedly and the controls were badly damaged, but he made two successful landings and rescued the last American on the ground. Major Brady had shown enough heroism for a lifetime, but his day was not yet over.

After trading in his bullet-riddled chopper for a better one, he faced one more mission—landing in an enemy minefield and bringing out a trapped platoon of U.S. soldiers. Several other pilots had tried to do this and all had failed,

A UH-1H helicopter rescuing injured soldiers in Vietnam.

Washington. The Knights of Columbus Lantern Award is reserved for men who give special meaning to Charity, Unity, Fraternity, and Patriotism—men like Brady, who stand as brilliant examples of serving one's country, one's fellow citizens, and the Catholic Church.

During his two tours of duty in Vietnam, Brady flew more than 2,000 combat missions and evacuated more than 5,000 wounded. It has been estimated that he single-handedly rescued more men than anyone else in the history of combat, demonstrating both courage and love beyond measure.

Since retiring from the military, Major General Brady, who holds an MBA degree from Notre Dame, has become the chairman of the Citizens Flag Alliance; he is a passionate supporter of an amendment to ban any desecration of the American flag.

but the Major was undeterred: he flew straight into the field and landed safely. But something or somebody detonated a mine near the chopper, wounding two of his crew members and damaging his aircraft. Despite the damage, he got the helicopter off the ground and flew six severely wounded patients to medical aid. At last, he was able to return to the base for the night. He was uninjured and would fly more missions as soon as he got some rest and a new chopper.

During this single day in Vietnam, Major Brady used three different helicopters to evacuate 51 men, many of whom would have died without him. The three choppers held more than 400 bullet holes and the flying skills he displayed in that fog in the jungles of Southeast Asia eventually earned him a place in military history and in the Army Aviation Hall of Fame. They were part of a record that brought him the Distinguished Service Cross, the Purple Heart, and the Congressional Medal of Honor for his "conspicuous gallantry and intrepidity in action."

Years later, Supreme Knight Carl A. Anderson presented Major General Brady with another honor, this one for his longtime dedication to the Catholic Church and the Knights of Columbus at Holy Disciples Council 11948 in Puyallup,

Major General Brady speaking at the Basilica of the National Shrine of the Immaculate Conception on the first anniversary of 9/11.

Blessed Carlos M. Rodríguez

There are many ways to actively engage in spiritual life. Some have written books on religious faith, others have volunteered as missionaries in faraway lands, and still others have ministered to soldiers during wartime. Carlos Rodríquez found a quieter path and gentler means of serving, but what he did for his Church changed people's lives. Rodríguez was a layman from Caguas, Puerto Rico, and little known outside his family and small community. Local people called him "Charlie" and never treated him formally because he was not a Catholic cleric. He was a member of Juan XXIII Council 2033 in Caguas, Puerto Rico, and remained a Knight until his death.

Born in 1918, he was one of five children from a very religious Catholic family. One sister became a Carmelite nun, and a brother became a Benedictine monk. Charlie was a loving and compassionate person even as a child, and he would not hesitate to help others, even if it put his own life in danger. At the age of nine, he saved his one-year-old cousin from a rabid dog. Though Charlie was injured in the attack, he had saved a life, and that made the experience worthwhile. His enthusiasm for service and love of the Church also motivated him to serve Mass regularly as an altar boy. At a time when the Mass was still in Latin, he often translated from Latin to Spanish so that everyone in the church could understand. At age 13, he began to suffer from a painful and incurable disease, ulcerative colitis, which eventually led to the rectal cancer that took his life when he was only 44. Despite how difficult his life often was, Charlie accepted his illness with grace. He never lost his faith, and he turned his pain and suffering into an inspiration for others. His infirmity was the gateway to his spiritual mission.

The sicker he became, the more eager he was to help others feel better through making a connection to God. A scholar of moral and religious matters, he constantly studied the Bible, looking for new insights. Then he shared with people what he had discovered about love, piety, and acceptance. He never stopped talking about his love of God, and he never stopped teaching. It was as natural to Charlie as breathing. Because he knew his time on earth was going to be limited, he was determined to use every waking minute in prayer or in helping others.

He was credited with invigorating the campus ministry at the University of Puerto Rico, but he wasn't heralded for his good works as much as for the example he set. He didn't just talk about love; it was apparent in everything he did. He didn't just promote faith; he personified it in the flesh. He didn't merely talk about Christ; he was a living witness to faith in the midst of adversity, and he followed in Christ's footsteps

Blessed Carlos Rodríguez (center) with a group of students from the University of Puerto Rico.

by picking up his cross without complaint. He didn't just pay lip service to the virtues extolled by the Knights of Columbus; he lived them on a daily basis. He published a magazine, *Christian Life Days*, to deepen the university students' appreciation for the seasons of the liturgical year. He started a group called the Christian Culture Circle at the Catholic University in Rio Piedras. At the University of Puerto Rico, he organized a chorus, and taught catechism. If there was a spiritual need in his Catholic community, Rodríguez was there to fill it.

Cancer took his life in July 1963, but not before he'd written down his thoughts about what he'd learned since the illness had struck him. His small book, *At That Time*, was penned in Spanish but has been translated into English, and it captured the core of Charlie's beliefs and experiences. It established him as a religious pioneer in the days before Vatican II, through his belief that the Church in Puerto Rico needed liturgical reform to reach out to more worshippers. He advocated the use of the vernacular and the full restoration of the "Paschal Vigil" to its central place in Church observances.

Charlie's death was very slow and painful, yet he never lost courage in the face of it. The cancer only deepened his faith and commitment to his own kind of ministry. In his last hours, he called upon the love of God and found its abundance within. When given the chance to feel sorry for himself, he spoke of others who'd suffered more. Even in

agony, he radiated the peace he found through Christ. His funeral was distinguished not by grief but by joy—the very same joy felt from him while he was alive.

In 1987, proclaimed as the "Year of the Laity" by John Paul II, Charlie's friends and relatives began promoting his cause as Puerto Rico's first saint. Many eyewitnesses have come forward with testimony about the depth of Charlie's faith and his practice of virtue. One woman was cured of cancer after asking his help in prayer. On December 20, 1999, Pope John Paul II paved the way for Charlie's beatification by signing a decree attributing this miracle to his intercession. The Knights of Columbus in Puerto Rico have promoted his cause, and in April 2001, Charlie became the first Puerto Rican to be beatified. More than 2000 Puerto Ricans flew to Rome to attend the ceremony. And in America, Knights in Kissimmee, Florida, have honored him as the namesake of Blessed Carlos Rodríguez Council 13116. This humble and faithful servant of the Church is certainly worthy of such recognition.

The beatification ceremony of Carlos Rodríguez, April 29, 2001.

John W. McCormack

When John Kennedy was assassinated in November 1963, John McCormack, the Speaker of the U.S. House of Representatives, was suddenly thrust into the spotlight. He was next in line to be president should anything happen to Kennedy's replacement, Vice President Lyndon Johnson. At the time, McCormack was 71, and some in Washington and elsewhere grumbled that in case of unexpected events, he was too old to be in the Oval Office. McCormack never responded to these complaints, but let others do his talking for him. The Massachusetts congressman had been in the House for 35 years and hardly needed to defend his record or accomplishments. He knew how his colleagues felt about him, and that was more important than all the carping about his age.

At Christmastime 1963, during a period of intense debate on the House floor, Florida Representative Charles E. Bennett rose and declared that it was a special moment in American politics. It was the middle of a heated all-night session in Congress, but it was also McCormack's 72nd birthday. One representative after another now stood to honor McCormack and wish him a happy birthday, but Congressman Bennett gave the crowning speech.

"Mr. Speaker," he said, "your birthday is an occasion for joy for everyone in the House, for we all love you. It is also an occasion which gives us the opportunity to demonstrate our great respect for the unparalleled service to your country...you have brought to this service a fighting Irish spirit and a universal concern for the progress and betterment of mankind, capped by a patriotism and dedication to our country which has no peer...we see in you the forbearance and sympathy, the perfect tolerance, which speaks eloquently of your Christian inspiration."

No words could have more accurately described the life and achievements and values of this Knight of Columbus.

McCormack was born in South Boston on December 21, 1891. The area was marked by poverty and by faith—it had produced more vocations for the priests and nuns than any other American community. John was one of twelve children. His father Joseph, a bricklayer, died of tuberculosis when the boy was completing the eighth grade. John had to quit school and help support his mother and siblings, but was determined to keep educating himself. After knocking around at a series of odd jobs, he was hired as an attorney's office boy, at $4 a week. The office stirred his ambition, and he spent every idle moment reading law books. At 21, he passed the Massachusetts bar and went into practice as a trial lawyer. He was successful but had the undeniable "itch and the urge," as he called it, to get into politics. He also wanted to become more involved in Catholicism and the Order. In 1917, he became a member of Père Marquette Council 271 in South Boston and was active there for decades. His faith would become an integral part of his political career, especially in his support of civil rights and minority causes. It was the foundation of his "perfect tolerance," as Congressman Bennett had put it.

McCormack was elected to the Massachusetts State House of Representatives in 1920, and to the state Senate in 1923 before running for and winning a U.S. Congressional seat in 1928. He was a natural political figure, who loved spending after-work hours with his professional friends playing poker and discussing legislative bills or other affairs of state. With a cigar clenched between his teeth and smoke billowing around his prominent head, he looked every inch the renowned and influential politician. He was soon given a seat on the powerful Ways and Means Committee—the first sophomore congressman ever to earn this distinction. After serving more than three decades in the House, he was finally elected to the Speaker's position in 1962, becoming the first Catholic to hold this post. Well suited to playing the role of arbiter and wise man on the often-contentious floor of the U.S. Congress, he was known for one thing above all. When he made a promise on a political matter, he held to it, whether he wanted to or not.

"Sometimes," he once said, "I wish I hadn't given my word but I must keep it. I say to myself, 'McCormack, if you were fool enough to give your word, you ought to be fool enough to keep it.'"

He knew how to bring people together and get things done—even when opposing factions were refusing to give an inch.

"The road to progress," he said, "is, in moments of contest, reasonable compromise. You don't compromise principles, but you harmonize tactics to preserve unity... I have never asked a member to vote against his conscience. If he mentions his conscience, that's all—I don't press him any further."

Following President Kennedy's assassination, McCormack continued to serve as Speaker of the House until his retirement in 1971. His popularity in his home state can be seen in several buildings that bear his name. In 1967, when a new public school was built in Dorchester, it was named after him; Dorchester had been part of the district McCormack had represented for so many years, and he had attended the public school when he was a boy. He was also honored in 1983 when the University of Massachusetts's Boston campus named an institute that studies political science after him, followed by the creation in 2003 of the John W. McCormack Graduate School of Policy Studies. McCormack was an Irish Catholic Knight very much in the Al Smith mold (see page 38), a man who went from childhood poverty to the highest levels of government and politics, armed with faith, a habit of reading voraciously to make up for the education he'd missed, and a natural talent for leading and inspiring those with whom he served.

John McCormack shakes hands with Knights of Columbus members.

Father Charles J. Watters

When Joe Watters was a boy in Rutherford, New Jersey, and attending a religion class in school, a nun asked him what he wanted to be when he grew up and without hesitating, he said, "A priest." Later that day, Joe relayed this story to his mother and told her about wanting to serve in the Church, but she dismissed his remarks. She thought her son had just been trying to impress the nun. Half a dozen years later, when Joe was in high school and being honored as a top student, he was called on stage and asked the same question: What did he want to do with the rest of his life?

"I want to be a Roman Catholic priest," he replied.

His family was starting to think he was serious. After attending Seton Hall University, he entered Immaculate Conception Seminary in New Jersey, and was ordained on May 30, 1953. He served parishes in several cities, including one in Rutherford. While receiving his religious training, he showed his penchant for adventure by taking flying lessons and joining the New Jersey Air National Guard. He put that experience to use in 1965, when he went on active duty as a chaplain in the U.S. Army. Although he was 38 years old, he volunteered to go to Vietnam and joined the 2nd Battalion, 173rd Airborne Brigade, known as the "Sky Soldiers." At heart this Knight from Regina Council 1688 of Rutherford, New Jersey, was a grunt and a paratrooper—jumping out of airplanes alongside the other men and marching through rice paddies armed with his Bible. He heard the confessions of the men in his brigade and always had his Mass kit at the ready. He loved being a part of a tight-knit outfit that was living on the edge of survival, and he loved the action and camaraderie. When his first tour of duty ended, he re-upped for another tour in Vietnam. He wanted to stay there until the war was over and all of "his boys" could come home.

On November 17, 1967, his task force's mission was to capture Hill 875, an obscure but well-defended encampment near the Cambodian border. The enemy was entrenched on Hill 875 and everyone knew that the fight would be bloody. That morning, just before the attack was to commence, Father Watters celebrated Mass. Normally, his service drew 20–30 men but today it brought in more than 100, including non-Catholics, and even those who professed not to have any faith. The task force seemed to sense that this was a critical moment. In fact, so many came to Mass that morning that Father Watters had to break the regular-sized host into many smaller pieces so that all could take Communion. He gave absolution, and then the fighting began.

One of Father Watters' favorite Biblical passages was John 15:13.

Father Watters prays during a baptism ceremony of soldiers in his unit.

"There is no greater love than this," it reads, "than to lay down one's life for one's friends."

As the Americans came under intense enemy fire that day in November 1967, Father Joe rushed forward to support them—still without a weapon—providing aid and anointing the wounded. He picked up one soldier who was in shock and carried him to safety, then rescued another fallen young man who could not crawl out of harm's way. He ran straight into a firefight to grab two paratroopers, and saved several more who lay wounded outside the line of defense. Once he'd dragged them back inside the safe zone, he put field bandages on them, gave them food and water, and offered them prayer and comfort. The battle raged all around him but Father Watters never missed a moment to serve his boys—until he was hit and crumbled to the ground, writhing in a pool of blood.

Moments later, he lay dead.

In the midst of the fighting, combat veterans gathered round him and began to cry for the loss of their spiritual leader. They simply could not believe that he'd been taken and it took them a few moments to realize they were still in the middle of a war. Then they went back into battle. A lot of men died that day on Hill 875 but no death was felt more deeply than this one. The soldiers were stunned by Father Joe's courage and sacrifice—his willingness to walk unarmed into gunfire to help save lives and carry out his sacramental duties. They were "his boys" and he'd been their light and inspiration to the very end.

For his work in Vietnam, Father Watters, who had achieved the rank of Major, was posthumously given the Congressional Medal of Honor in November of 1969, only the fourth Catholic priest ever to receive this award. He is buried in Arlington National Cemetary. In 2002, the Knights of Columbus teamed with the New Jersey Vietnam Veterans Memorial Foundation to honor him with a Fourth Degree Exemplification. On that occasion, another Vietnam veteran, Past Faithful Navigator Jerry Spanola of Our Lady of Lourdes Assembly, said, "Jesus laid down his life for us on Calvary, and Father Watters laid down his life for his friends on Hill 875 in Vietnam."

Joe Watters, priest and paratrooper, Knight and chaplain, loved God, his vocation and his fellow men, and he died doing what he believed in—serving others and serving his country.

The men of the 173rd Airborne Brigade honor fallen comrades who were killed on Hill 875.

Joseph A. Sullivan

Few people outside professional law enforcement circles knew that Joe Sullivan was regarded as the most effective law enforcement officer in our history. Many of his brothers in the Knights of Columbus knew of Sullivan's accomplishments, but also respected his modesty and insistence that he was simply fortunate—and proud—to be on two great teams: the Federal Bureau of Investigation and the Knights of Columbus.

One reason for his relative obscurity is that it didn't pay to make headlines under J. Edgar Hoover, the legendary and controversial head of the FBI, who led the bureau from 1924 until his death in 1972. Hoover loved the spotlight, so Sullivan learned how to survive the internal politics of the FBI. He investigated everything from killings to espionage, and from fraud to civil rights violations, but he did it quietly and discreetly.

The FBI was the perfect place for Sullivan to work to make a difference, especially in the area of civil rights. As a young man, Joe's father, George, had been the target of a KKK campaign to remove him as principal of a school in Hurley, Wisconsin, simply because he was Catholic. George Sullivan had already been prevented from getting a teaching job in the state of New York, despite his excellent grades in college, for the same reason.

The personal experiences with bigotry—and the stories told about his Irish immigrant grandfather who had escaped from a British "coffin ship"—gave him a lifelong revulsion towards prejudice.

A Wisconsin native, Joe attended the University of Wisconsin in Madison, where he played football for the Badgers. To help pay for his education, he worked in an iron ore mine. He graduated in 1938 and then went on for a law degree. A fellow Wisconsin alumnus told him of an opening at the FBI. With World War II raging on two fronts, Joe served the FBI as a member of the Special Investigative Services (SIS) and was sent to Venezuela to shadow Nazi agents there. After the war, Joe came back to the United States, and was assigned to a variety of posts around the country.

Despite his efforts to keep a low profile in deference to Hoover, Sullivan became the stuff of legend by inadvertently upstaging his boss. One weekend, Sullivan found himself the darling of the media when the New York Bureau, which he headed, announced the cracking of a case involving hundreds of truck hijackings by the Mafia. It was a case that Hoover had not thought to make into a media event.

Through no fault of his own, Sullivan made the headlines, and soon found himself "promoted" to a field office in Alaska. In Anchorage, where he became Special Agent in Charge, Sullivan helped found Our Lady of the Snows Council 4859, along with some of the other parishioners. He was now a member of two organizations, the FBI and the Knights, for which he had a great love. And whenever he traveled or was off duty at home, he would seek out the fellowship to be found at the local Knights of Columbus Hall.

Hoover eventually brought Sullivan back from Alaska to Washington, D.C., and made him Major Case Inspector in 1962. With the number of cases that Sullivan had to handle in quick succession, he soon became known around the Bureau as "a one-man flying squad."

In 1963, Joe was involved in an investigation of organized crime in Cleveland that helped expose the mob's use of Las Vegas for money laundering. In 1964, he investigated union violence and corruption in Florida. Sullivan was put in charge of the operation, and while chasing bombing suspects there, he came upon a bomb set to detonate when the next train came by. Having worked briefly as a miner, and knowing his way around explosives, Sullivan was able to disable the bomb. Hoover reprimanded him because a suspect had escaped while Sullivan disabled the bomb, but the train crew was certainly grateful.

During the civil rights battles in the 1960s, Sullivan was sent to the deep South. When three civil rights workers were kidnapped and killed in June 1964, with the collusion of the local law enforcement authorities, President Johnson ordered Hoover and the FBI to take action. Sullivan responded to the call, and worked on the murder cases for months in the face of open hostility from local police agencies.

The fire-gutted wreck of the kidnapped activists' car was eventually found, after an informant's tip. And another informant, whose identity Joe Sullivan kept secret for the rest of his life, told him where to find the bodies on a farm in Mississippi.

Although he had worked on lots of important cases over the years, involving everything from the Mafia to Nazi agents in South America, Joe Sullivan always felt that the FBI's greatest achievements—and his—were the civil rights investigations carried out in the 1960s.

Throughout the rest of his career, when the Bureau had a special assignment, Hoover would usually growl: "Get me Sullivan." And before retiring, Joe Sullivan headed up several more high-profile cases, including one that took him back to his alma mater: the 1970 bombing of the University of Wisconsin's Army Math Research Center by a radical group called the Weathermen. A physics researcher named Robert Fassnacht was killed in the blast. Joe was able to solve the case in only a week and a half.

After retiring from the FBI, Joe devoted his remaining years to charity, the first principle of the Knights of Columbus. He won a Humanitarian Service Award for his work with the homeless in New York City. He was an active parishioner at St. Agnes Catholic Church near Grand Central Station. Only weeks before his death from prostate cancer on August 2, 2002, Sullivan could be found keeping order in the soup kitchen or sweeping up the dining hall.

Joe Sullivan exemplified charity, unity, fraternity, and patriotism as few have. He was a credit to his country, the FBI, and the Knights of Columbus.

NOTE: Information for this profile was provided by Tom Pison, Joe Sullivan's friend and biographer, who is now writing a book on Sullivan's life entitled *Get Sullivan*. People with information and stories about Joe Sullivan are invited to contact Tom Pison at tap2@verizon.net

REVIEW & OUTLOOK

The Gentle G-Man

Not many men played by Gene Hackman could claim to be larger in real life. But Joseph Aloysius Sullivan was not most men. When he died last Friday at the age of 85, the FBI lost one of its legends.

In "Mississippi Burning"—a fictionalized account of how the FBI solved the 1964 murder of three civil-rights activists—Mr. Hackman's character was a composite loosely based on Sullivan, who solved the murders in the teeth of hostility from Klan-infested Mississippi police forces. In Hollywood's version, Hackman even beats up a local deputy in a barber shop.

But within the FBI family, Sullivan was known for brains more than brawn. A University of Wisconsin football player who caught the eye of sportswriter Red Smith, the burly, cigar-smoking Sullivan opted for the FBI instead of the gridiron. He started character, "Joe didn't get physical—he got professional." The case started to break when Sullivan, using a tip from an informant, led diggers out to a dam on a farm and poked a stick in the ground; the bodies were found only a few feet away.

"That he had been so accurate scared the living daylights out of the Klan," says Mr. Martin. "Because they thought that when they buried those boys they would never be found." Ultimately Sullivan helped convict seven people on federal civil-rights charges, because the state of Mississippi either wouldn't prosecute or wouldn't convict on murder. Mr. Martin describes Mississippi in those days as a police state within America, where blacks were terrorized by a law-enforcement and legal community that was in cahoots with the night riders.

Obituary of Joseph Sullivan, from the Wall Street Journal, *August 9, 2002.*

John W. McDevitt

John W. McDevitt was the consummate Boston Irish Catholic—with all that implies. He was passionate about the Catholic faith, and he deeply loved his country. And as was the case with John F. Kennedy, his election signaled an important generational change.

An educator by profession, John McDevitt was the man chosen to lead the Order during the harrowing and turbulent 1960s and '70s. No one before or since has been presented with quite the same volatile combination of issues that he faced.

McDevitt was the first Supreme Knight to be born in the 20th century, in December, 1906 in Malden, Massachusetts.

He graduated from Boston College in 1928 and earned a masters degree a year later. For two decades he was superintendent of schools in Waltham, Massachusetts, and then served as chairman of the state's Board of Education. In 1960 he was elected Deputy Supreme Knight and became Supreme Knight shortly after the death of Luke Hart in February of 1964.

As soon as he took office, McDevitt confronted issues that were roiling American society in general and the Catholic church in particular. The Knights of Columbus annual convention met in New Orleans just six weeks after President Johnson signed the Civil Rights Act of 1964, and just days before the convention was to begin, McDevitt was informed that the hotel intended to enforce its policy of barring blacks. He sent word that the convention would move to another hotel if the policy wasn't changed. McDevitt and the Knights won, and made a point of putting a black priest, Father Harold Perry, at the head table for the States Dinner, a highlight of the annual gathering. McDevitt also led the successful effort to change the Order's "blackball" rules, which were being used in some councils to keep blacks out.

The following year, he arranged for the Knights to join with Hartford Archbishop Henry O'Brien in co-sponsoring a conference on human rights, focusing on racial justice. In 1966, McDevitt urged convention delegates to support "efforts to shake the country free from any prejudice...to create conditions which will give every American a chance to obtain decent housing...to eliminate the causes of poverty... and to foster interreligious and interracial understanding." In 1969, at McDevitt's urging, the Knights of Columbus pledged $75,000 to the U.S. Catholic Conference Task Force on Urban Problems. The funds went toward confronting and healing the persistent ills of discrimination and poverty.

The mid-1960s were also a period in which the entire Catholic church began to implement the changes brought about by the Second Vatican Council. The council had a dramatic impact on the Catholic Church, one that continues to be felt today. Its purpose was a renewal of the church, but there were many who saw it as an invitation to revolution. It brought about many positive changes, such as allowing Mass to be said in the vernacular and encouraging Catholics to participate in interfaith dialogue; but it was also accompanied by an unsettling drop in vocations, and the changes in the liturgy were difficult for many to absorb.

McDevitt rejected the notion that the Order had to join one camp or the other. "Is the Knights of Columbus a conservative or a progressive society?" he asked at the 1967 convention. "We are both progressive and conservative and we are neither." The Knights were progressive in their "efforts to shake the country free from any prejudice" and "to create conditions which will give every American a chance to obtain decent money." But progressivism based on "enchantment with the popular idea of change as such" was another matter entirely. Nor would the order embrace "the static philosophy of traditionalism." Knights would be defined by their loyalty to the bishops and the Pope, recognizing their responsibility for "teaching, sanctifying, and guiding the Church." That meant adhering to church teaching on everything from birth control, abortion and divorce to matters of social justice. For his loyalty and his leadership, Pope Paul VI honored him in 1965 by naming him a Knight Commander of the Order of Saint Gregory, one of several awards and honors he would receive from the Pope over the next decade. And in 1976, his alma mater, Boston College, recognized his distinguished career by giving him an honorary Doctorate of Laws.

Speaking at a Knights convention in 1966, McDevitt said that it was time for Catholics and Knights to recognize that they had finally succeeded in overcoming the prejudice that hung over them for so long, and they should now act accordingly. He recalled that in decades past, the Knights of Columbus had "served principally as a fortress where members could gather and feel mutual encouragement and strength against the slings of a society still hostile to both their religion and their nationality." By the 1960s, however, the Church had "become the leading Christian body in the land…It is high time we abandon the concept of our Order as mainly a fortress to protect us from a hostile world. We are not a besieged minority."

John McDevitt was also a pivotal figure in bringing modern communication capabilities to the Holy See. He engineered the donation of one of two new short-wave transmitters to the Vatican (the second one came from Francis Cardinal Spellman of New York). Then in 1975, the Order began funding satellite television uplinks from the Vatican, so that the Pope would now be able to deliver live telecasts from St. Peter's Basilica to the faithful all over the globe. Under McDevitt, the Order built its 22-story headquarters in New Haven, with four corner towers symbolizing the four principles of the Knights of Columbus. Fittingly enough, it fell to McDevitt to define anew the principles of Charity, Unity, Fraternity, and Patriotism at a time when everything everywhere was being questioned. In the 1960s, the Order needed a renewed clarity of purpose. It found the right man for the job, someone with the necessary combination of appreciating the past and building for the future.

Dr. Christopher Kauffman, Knights of Columbus historian and Professor of American Church History at the Catholic University in Washington, D.C., described McDevitt as a "broker of consensus who, nonetheless, was not reluctant to take a firm position on issues." The Order would emerge from the 60s stronger than ever and prepared for the decades to come. As Supreme Knight, McDevitt had walked the fine line of change without losing his balance, moving the organization through the eye of that needle.

John McDevitt meets with Knights and community leaders about promoting civil rights, 1965.

CHAPTER SIX

The 1970s & 1980s

Harry E. McKillop

At the end of the 1960s, Harry McKillop, a successful business associate of Ross Perot, began looking for a new challenge that engaged other parts of his intelligence, creativity, humanity, and spirituality. He wanted to use the impulse to help others that had been nurtured by his Catholic upbringing. He searched and searched until finding his special mission—locating and bringing home American POWs from all over Southeast Asia.

The first call came into Ross Perot's office in Texas in the early '70s, just as Saigon was falling to the Communist North Vietnamese. "Max" Dat Nguyen, a former South Vietnamese Air Force colonel, had been arrested and was being held by the Viet Cong at an embassy compound. Perot's colleagues, including McKillop, were told that three former American POWs were willing to risk their lives by attempting to rescue their wartime ally. Perot immediately phoned a White House official who called the Saigon Embassy, which set things in motion. The Americans were able to free Max and 32 members of his family before Vietnamese Communists retook the compound.

Subsequently, McKillop agreed to help Perot rescue a group of Vietnamese Nung people who'd escaped to China but had been imprisoned by Chinese authorities on High Island. If they tried to reenter Vietnam, they faced certain death. This time Perot's efforts to work with the American government were rebuffed, but the Texan was a very determined and resourceful man. He contacted McKillop and asked if he'd be willing to lead a team to carry out the rescue. The answer was an unequivocal yes. McKillop quickly put together a group including Nguyen that traveled to High Island, stormed the prison, and, using a set of dramatic maneuvers, freed 175 Nungs.

"I still don't know exactly how they got them off that island," Mr. Perot later told the media. "Harry won't tell me. Maybe it's best I don't know."

After carrying out other successful missions in Vietnam, Laos, and Cambodia, McKillop was ready to expand his efforts beyond Southeast Asia. In 1979, two American executives employed in Iran by EDS were picked up and jailed by Islamic revolutionaries who had taken power there. Perot hired a Green Beret legend, Colonel Arthur "Bull" Simons, to plot a breakout strategy at the prison, and McKillop was a member of Bull's planning team. Using envelopes stuffed with cash to grease the wheels and to initiate protest riots around the jail compound, the team was able to free both prisoners in a high-risk escapade that miraculously left no one hurt. With this experience to build on, McKillop would go on to coordinate the liberation of people held captive in Mexico, Turkey, and Saudi Arabia, becoming nearly as legendary in the rescue business as Bull Simons himself.

In the 1980s, Perot received a call from an American businessman who'd learned of an elderly American woman held prisoner in China for more than four decades. At the start of World War II, she was the daughter of a wealthy family living in China. The Japanese had captured her, labeled her an enemy combatant, and thrown her in jail. When the war ended, the Japanese jailers went home, but the Chinese prison guards who replaced them claimed that she was working for the CIA, and refused to release her. Years passed and no one tried to help her.

The businessman phoning Perot had managed to snap a picture of the front gate of the prison where she was locked up, but was uncertain of the address. With only these details to go on, and with considerable resistance from the Chinese government, McKillop flew to China and scoured the city and countryside looking for the prison. He finally found a prison gate matching the photo and then talked his way inside the jail. There was Marjorie Fuller, who'd been a POW—in World War II and throughout the Cold War—for more than forty years. McKillop negotiated with the Chinese authorities as a medical consultant to arrange her release to his custody in the United States. She was flown back to America and eventually moved into a nursing home in Baltimore.

Entering the United States for the first time, Marjorie said, "I had a miracle happen. God brought me home for Christmas, my Irish boyfriend."

McKillop said that his faith sustained him through his heroic undertakings. "I believe that you have to believe and the accomplishments fall into place," he said.

In 2003, to honor McKillop's heroic efforts over the past 30 years, Ross Perot initiated the "Harry McKillop Irish Spirit Award." It was designed to recognize a person of Irish or Irish-American descent who'd shown unusual commitment and valor in helping those in need. The first recipient of the $25,000 award was Mrs. Jean Kelly, Founder and Director of the Speedwell Trust of Northern Ireland. In 1991, the Trust began as a volunteer organization working

for peace and reconciliation. Mrs. Kelly labored tirelessly to bring Catholic and Protestant children together in schools and Northern Ireland communities, where they were given the chance to interact in a safe environment and develop greater respect and understanding for one another. Every year, 20,000 kids and adults participated in this kind of education. The endeavor had a very personal component for Mrs. Kelly, a Protestant who'd married a Catholic man. Personally and professionally, she'd devoted her life to healing the divisions between the two groups in her homeland.

McKillop, a former Grand Knight of New World Council 9903 in McKinney, Texas, had joined the Knights of Columbus at his father Harry Sr.'s urging back in Brooklyn, New York, where he grew up. Active involvement in the Knights became a lifelong passion. Despite the stresses of flying around the world to rescue those whom no one else could help, McKillop still managed to make most of his Knights of Columbus meetings. "I used to go to meetings within two hours of returning from the Far East," he explained. McKillop said the camaraderie of the Knights, and the Order's principles were what drew him in. Even in his eighties, McKillop could still be found attending Knights functions.

Harry McKillop (left) with Jean Kelly, the first recipient of the Harry McKillop Irish Spirit Award, and Ross Perot.

Ronald A. Guidry

In the summer of 1978, some of the New York Yankees were losing their composure and their tempers. Conflict was everywhere. Star outfielder Reggie Jackson was quarreling with team leader and catcher Thurman Munson. Owner George Steinbrenner expected the Yanks to repeat as World Series champions, and became publicly upset whenever they lost a couple of games in a row. Manager Billy Martin was fighting with Steinbrenner and would not survive the season on the job. Throughout the first few months of the '78 season, the team was in disarray. By the All-Star break in mid-July, they had fallen a seemingly insurmountable fourteen games behind their most hated rival in the American League East Division, the Boston Red Sox. Fans everywhere were saying

it was Boston's year at last. The Yanks were going to be dethroned and the Sox were going to win the World Series.

More than ever, the Yankees needed a rock, someone to steady them when things were about to collapse. One player on the team had grown up in the South, surrounded by the values of Catholicism. Ron Guidry had always had something extra to lean on, quietly using his faith and his family to help focus himself as a professional athlete— never letting himself get too high or too low. The game was what was important, the focal point was the team, not the individual. Guidry would need his faith early in the 1978 season, when he was the only reason the Yanks did not entirely fall apart. Known to fans as "Louisiana Lightning," this left-hander was about to show the baseball world something it had never before witnessed. Almost single-handedly, he held the team together, winning game after game to keep the Yanks in contention. The unassuming young Southerner, who always stayed close to his religious roots, was arguably the best hurler in the game.

In April, May, and June, he won his first 13 decisions in a row and threw nine shutouts for the season. His earned run average of 1.74 tied him with Sandy Koufax as the lowest for a left-hander since 1933. During July and August, he kept winning until the other Yankee pitchers started to come alive, the team's bats woke up, and the New Yorkers began to chip away at the Red Sox lead. By the first week of September, thanks mostly to Ron Guidry, the two teams were in a dead heat for the division lead.

As Guidry's accomplishments became more spectacular, he stayed out of the spotlight, going about his life as he always had, practicing his faith and taking care of his team. He didn't look particularly strong, but he was, as they say in his part of America, wound awfully tight. He had that mysterious thing baseball experts call a "live arm," meaning that he threw harder than most other pitchers, and his curveball broke so much that hitters had trouble seeing it.

Every four days the Yankees could count on him to deliver a victory and he almost always did, but that wasn't enough to put away the feisty Red Sox. After both teams had played all 162 regular season games, each had won 99 and lost 63. Nothing had been settled so they scheduled a one-game playoff to decide the race.

Guidry started, of course, and did what he'd been doing all year long. He won his 25th game of the season in a dramatic come-from-behind victory, with the Yankees defeating the Red Sox on Bucky Dent's legendary left-field home run in Boston's Fenway Park. The Yanks had just completed the greatest comeback in the history of baseball, and Guidry had set a record of his own. He went 25-3 for the season, giving him the best winning percentage ever (.893) for a pitcher with 20 or more decisions. And he wasn't finished.

In the playoffs that year, Guidry won two games against the Kansas City Royals to clinch the pennant, and the Yanks then faced the Los Angeles Dodgers in the World Series. The two teams hadn't met in the Fall Classic since 1963, when the Dodgers had swept the Yankees, and it looked as if the pattern would now repeat itself. Los Angeles won the first two games but the New Yorkers took the next four in a row, Guidry himself winning two of those contests. The Yanks were again world champs and had achieved something that many veteran baseball watchers had considered impossible.

There has never been, before or since, a season to equal this one by the Cajun phenomenon: he showed everybody what grace under pressure and pitching perfection look like. While his celebrity teammates squabbled, the quiet southpaw kept shutting down the opposition. It was no wonder that he was given the Cy Young award, as baseball's best pitcher, that year. When the limelight eventually faded and Guidry retired from baseball in 1989, he went back home and concentrated on the values he relied upon as a pro athlete. In 1993, he became a member of the Assumption of the Virgin Mary Council 7411 in Mire, Louisiana.

He acted at the Council just as he had with the Yankees—eager to do his part but just as eager to stay away from the spotlight. He went to Knights' sponsored softball tournaments and helped make the events a success.

He autographed balls for kids and organized coaching hitting and pitching clinics. He built a ball diamond behind his home for local youngsters to have a place to play. He liked being with the other Knights, but not being singled out for any special recognition because of his renowned past.

"He's always willing to get involved with our projects," said Council 7411 Grand Knight Glen Meche, "but shies away from attention. His work with the Knights and with his family is a real expression of his faith. Ron's brother, Travis, is mentally disabled and a lot of his time goes to assisting him. Ron takes him bowling every Monday night and does other things with him other nights of the week. He's always there for his brother and will do anything he can to help."

In sports, fame and fortune come and go, but the foundation of a life in service to others is unchangeable. Yankee fans still are grateful for what Ron Guidry achieved and what he brought to the team; in 2003, the Yankees retired the number 49 that he wore. Always humble, he had tears in his eyes as he thanked his father and his teammates for having inspired him. Ron Guidry continues to exemplify a life of service and faith, whether he is in the public eye or not.

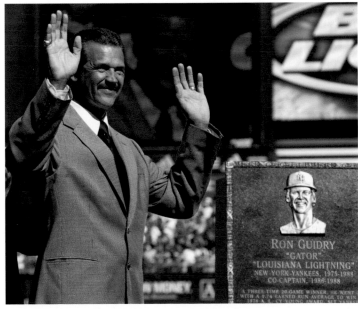

Ron Guidry waves to his fans as his uniform number is retired. Guidry's plaque is placed alongside other Yankee greats in Monument Park in Yankee Stadium.

Hilario G. Davide, Jr.

Around the globe, the rule of law is one of the essential foundations of a free and humane society. In peaceful times, the rule of law can often be taken for granted, but when trouble arrives, brave and principled people must have the courage to defend it. Since World War II, the Philippines has seen its share of political turmoil, particularly with the 20-year reign of Ferdinand Marcos. Filipinos have had to fight for democratic freedoms,

for legitimate elections, and for a legal system untainted by corruption. No one has done more than Hilario Davide, Jr. to make these ideals a part of Filipino life.

Nothing has come easily to this country or this man. Born December 20, 1935, in a mountain barrio in Argao, Cebu Province, he was one of seven children born to parents who were both teachers. He walked barefoot to school, and worked long hours as a teenager to save money for his education. He paid his way though the University of the Philippines by cleaning out dormitories. As a college student, he lacked the money to buy books, so at night he stayed in the library until it closed at 11 P.M., reading mostly about history and law. His grades were excellent, and after graduating in 1959, he gradually became known as a legal scholar, preparing himself to serve his country in ways that had not yet become clear. By the 1960s, he'd passed the bar and begun his career as an attorney.

A decade later, with the Marcos regime smothering the young democracy, he could not stay out of the political fray. He represented Cebu Province at the 1971 Constitutional Convention and when Marcos declared martial law in the Philippines, Davide challenged him head on. As an Assemblyman, he mobilized other Filipinos to offer resistance, calling for an end to martial law and sponsoring numerous bills that opposed government corruption and demanded election reforms.

It was during that tumultuous period that he became a Knight, and it was a life-changing event. Years later, during the Knights of Columbus centennial in the Philippines in 2005, Davide recalled: "One of the most memorable moments in my life was my admission, some thirty years ago, to the Knights of Columbus in the Philippines through the Father Matias Lucero Council No. 6054 in Argao, Cebu. It was a moment of transformation for me that changed the course of my life." He explained that "since that time, I felt that no day unfolded and ended in the same way as the previous ones. Every day was unique. No day ended in a sunset, but in the dawn of a new one enriched by faith, hope, and love."

In 1986, following the People Power Revolution that ousted Marcos and replaced him with President Corazon Aquino, Davide became a member of the Constitutional Commission. He played a key role in restoring democracy to the Philippines, drawing on his legal background to write the governing articles for the new legislature. He penned one truly remarkable sentence in those articles that revealed his longstanding passion for environmental law: "The State shall protect and advance the right of people to a balanced and healthful ecology in accord with the rhythm and harmony of nature."

He became the head of the Commission on Elections, and led formal investigations into military efforts to overthrow the new government. The elections that took place under Davide's leadership were considered among the fairest the country had ever held. In 1991, he was appointed to the Supreme Court of the Philippines. He believed in a strict interpretation of the law but remained deeply sensitive to environmental issues. In one landmark case, he supported the right of Filipino children and "generations yet unborn" to live in a healthy habitat and his ruling helped save 800,000 hectares of virgin rain forest. His crowning achievement came in December 1998 when he was made the Chief Justice of the Supreme Court. From that position he disciplined judges who violated their oath of office and brought mediation into Filipino courtrooms. He wanted transparency in all aspects of government and gave the rule of law in the Philippines a sense of decorum and respect. The barefoot boy from Cebu had come a very long way indeed, but had never forgotten his humble beginnings.

As Chief Justice he was presented with an award in Cebu on the 430th anniversary celebration of that province. It honored him for being an "outstanding" citizen and at the ceremony he revealed his heartfelt connection to his roots, his belief in the dignity of all Filipinos, and his unfailing democratic spirit. This award, he said, was not for his own pleasure but for the "other men and women of Cebu who gave their utmost for the greater glory of Cebu, country and God." It was for "the fishermen who protect our marine resources, the policemen who stay up late at night, and the spiritual leaders and teachers who sacrifice for our children's future despite the inadequate compensation. They are outstanding in themselves."

Well into his sixties, Davide still works long days and nights as Chief Justice, tirelessly hearing cases and writing opinions. In 2002, he received the Ramon Magsaysay Award for Government Service, in recognition of his commitment to democracy and the rule of law in the Philippines. Since childhood, this lifelong Catholic and past Grand Knight of the Saint Michael Council 6054 in Cebu City has drawn upon his spiritual foundation every step of his career. Taking the lessons of faith and family that he learned from his parents, he is a devoted husband and the father of five children. He has served as State Warden for the Knights, and as a member of the finance board of the Archdiocese of Cebu. Davide views his work in the courtroom as a vocation. He once summed up his view of being Chief Justice in six unforgettable words. "Administering justice," he said, "is a sacramental task."

Supreme Knight Carl Anderson and Hilario Davide.

Alfred F. "Bud" Jetty

The tensions that exist between the Native American community and mainstream U.S. society are historical and deep. For generations, it was difficult for either side to establish a relationship with the other based on mutual interest, respect, and trust, but a few brave people have been willing to step into this painful gap and make a difference.

Born April 7, 1933, on what is now called the Spirit Lake Indian Reservation in North Dakota, Bud Jetty took elementary school classes at the Indian Mission School in St. Michael, North Dakota, before going on to graduate from high school at St. Paul's Mission in Marty, South Dakota. In his formative years, the young Native American had extensive contact with Catholic culture, absorbing the beliefs, values, and history of the church. After serving in the U.S. Marine Corps, he returned to South Dakota with one overriding ambition: he wanted to bring about a reconciliation between contemporary American society and the Native American peoples. It was a huge task and one that most people would have seen as overwhelming, if not impossible. But Bud was a patient man with a long-term vision, and he set about working toward his goal every day of his life, while taking care of his family and other responsibilities.

In the mid-1970s, Jetty sought to fill a vacancy in the post of Hyde County Clerk-Magistrate. The Presiding Judge of the Sixth Circuit in South Dakota, Robert A. Miller, conducted an intensive search for the right candidate, and decided that Bud was the man for the job. Judge Miller selected him and put him in charge of all court records and magistrate work for the county. Bud turned out to be the perfect choice.

"Bud has not only performed his court duties efficiently and with the highest degree of integrity," wrote Sixth Circuit Judge Patrick J. McKeever in 1993, "but has, with dedication to his wife, family, church, community, and neighbors, also enhanced the reputation of the system he serves during his non-working hours."

Bud and Frances Jetty raised three kids of their own and took in two foster children from a troubled family. Bud joined the Knights of Columbus and rose through its ranks, seeing his mission with the Order the same way he'd seen his mission in life: he hoped to use the influence and prestige of the Knights to help bridge the divide between the two worlds he'd lived in since birth. The Order had the moral authority to lead the way for this reconciliation.

Jetty eventually became State Deputy for South Dakota, and in that capacity came to the attention of many Catholic officials, including Father Stanislaus Maudlin, OSB.

"I've been a Missionary among Dakotas and Chippewas since 1939," Father Maudlin wrote in 1992. "I've seen that each new generation has to be re-evangelized. Bias and self-advantage are staples in our daily diet for the young in schools. Weaning men/women away from such a diet is the long-time work of ministry. In our State, under the leadership of Mr. Jetty, the Knights are making great contributions to the proper mix of the gospel message…Alfred will bring a spirituality and an energy for evangelization that will make the Church even more proud than they are now of the men among us."

As State Deputy of the Knights of Columbus, Bud was known as an innovator. He organized exchanges between Indian and non-Indian schools, a program funded nationally by the Knights of Columbus. Urban students from around South Dakota came to Native American reservations for a different kind of education, while Indian kids made similar visits to city schools. All of them were actively involved in closing the gap between the two cultures, while learning things they could not have discovered by staying home.

On October 12, 1992, Bud could look on proudly as South Dakota embraced his vision and observed "Reconciliation Day" across the state. Amid Native American dancing and drumbeats at the Sioux Falls Coliseum, Governor George S. Mickelson celebrated the occasion by urging chambers of commerce, community clubs, and other organizations throughout South Dakota to set up citizen committees dedicated to spreading the idea of reconciliation and racial harmony.

The activities that day included a proclamation signed by the governor and tribal representatives, as well as a special tribute to Bud Jetty. "Reconciliation Day" was the culmination of everything he'd been working for throughout the past four decades—on the job, with his family, and in the Knights of Columbus. For all his efforts in trying to heal these historical wounds, Bud was given a citation written by Ben Black Bear, Jr., Chairman of the Council for Reconciliation.

"In appreciation," it read, "of your individual efforts to bring understanding of cultures through education and communication in South Dakota." And given his many accomplishments, it is not surprising that Bud was also inducted into the South Dakota Hall of Fame in 2003.

In addition to everything he has done to foster greater respect for Native Americans, Bud's love for his Catholic faith remains strong: in 2001, he was ordained a deacon, and continues to be active at St. James Church in Chamberlain, South Dakota. He enjoys his work with the Knights, and volunteers his time visiting local hospitals to bring comfort to those who need it. Bud Jetty has never let anything deter him, no matter how difficult or how challenging things may have appeared. His motto seems to be "the impossible isn't really impossible—it just takes a little longer to achieve."

Painting that was presented to St. Joseph's Indian School on Reconciliation Day.

Matthew C. Gannon

In the mid-1960s, Matthew Gannon and his wife, Miriam, decided to have a bigger family, but not in the usual way. They already had a daughter, but wanted to do something for kids without parents, and hoped to start adopting. Matthew himself had been orphaned at sixteen and was always concerned when he met children who had no parents of their own. For years, he'd wished he could do something about this, but the circumstances were never right. Now that he was nearing fifty, he decided to act.

Matthew, who worked for a Ford dealership in Braintree, Massachusetts, and later ran his own TV repair business, faced one potential problem: he looked more like a grandfather than a father. His hair was graying and he was fearful that an adoption agency might think he was too old to be a good parent to a young boy or girl. A friend told him about a hair product that combined dye and conditioner, which

would turn his locks brown and knock at least 20 years off his appearance. Matthew was so eager to go forward with his adoption plans that he immediately drove to the store and bought the treatment. After putting on the conditioner and rubbing it in, he glanced in the mirror and was startled.

"My hair had turned red," he says, "and I looked like Bozo the clown. I called the guy who'd recommended this and he started laughing. He said don't worry about it. Just rinse if off and put on the dye and you'll be fine. I did and he was right."

Now Matthew had brown hair but a gray mustache. There was only one solution—the facial hair had to go before he and Miriam went in to adopt. Knowing that he was serving a bigger cause than vanity, he marched into the bathroom and shaved it off.

The strategy must have worked because the couple soon brought home a little boy. They liked having him so much that they went back for more—and then more, and then more. By the mid-'70s, they'd either adopted or become foster parents to thirteen kids. They had a small house, at least at the start, but Matthew was handy with tools and a talented repairman, and the residence was now growing with the size of his family. Every time he brought a new child home, he either thought about building another addition or got out his tools. Some of the children took only weeks or months to adopt but one took six years. Time did not matter and neither did money (Matthew had a government pension on top of his regular job). When he and Miriam made a commitment to having a child live with them, they followed through until the process was completed, even if they had to hire lawyers to make it happen.

With at least a dozen kids in tow, Matthew started a summer ritual, packing all of them into a big trailer and heading across the country to Disneyland. The journey took several weeks round-trip, but that didn't matter, either.

Matthew had talked the Ford dealership into giving him time off and away he went ("If they'd told me no," he once explained, "I'd have quit the job.") One year he hauled seventeen children to Disneyland and back. Regardless of how much chaos or how many road challenges the journey presented, it was always worth it just to see the expressions on the kids' faces when they finally reached their destination in Anaheim.

A number of the children the Gannons adopted had serious disabilities. One girl was blind and others needed a wheelchair-friendly ramp and a special elevator to get up and down the floors. Matthew installed one himself. His house had grown from 24-feet-by-30-feet to 64-feet-by-64-feet, and it now had ten bedrooms. When he decided the kids would enjoy a swimming pool, he built one in the backyard. It cost $100,000 but he would pay if off eventually. By 2004, Matthew was 82 years old, but he and Miriam still had nine kids living under their roof. They also had 20 grandchildren who often came to visit. Their family reunions spilled out onto the street. Among the youngsters they'd raised were a nurse, a master plumber, the owner of a computer company, and a teacher of children with mental handicaps. Three worked in medical fields and two in food services. At 82, Matthew spent part of every day raising children.

In 1993, the Knights of Columbus began selecting a "Family of the Year" and in 2000, the Gannons were the unanimous choice for the award. They were given $10,000, which they promptly used on another cross-country trek to Disneyland with a trailer full of grateful children. By now, they'd adopted a total of 26 children and had been foster parents to 50 more. Matthew's concern for parentless children had impacted scores of lives.

"Life," he told everyone who asked him about the countless difficulties of raising such a large family, "has been very good to Miriam and me. The children keep us young and connected to so many different things. I never saw it as

work. Our only goal was to help as many kids as we could and doing this has brought me joy every single day."

Today, despite their age, the Gannons show no signs of slowing down—in fact, as of this writing, they still have 11 children living with them—ranging in age from 9 to 40!

Matthew Gannon holding the Memorial Award presented to him by the Massachusetts State Council.

Chris Godfrey

In 1980, after completing his senior year on the University of Michigan football team as a defensive lineman, Chris Godfrey wasn't drafted by any team in the National Football League. He had been a high school star at Detroit De La Salle, and played in three Rose Bowls as a college player, so he had expected that a professional team would be interested. Not being drafted was a terrible disappointment, but he was determined to impress the Washington Redskins with a free agent tryout. They signed him, but then cut him, and so he tried out with the New York Jets. But the next year, he injured his knee and the Jets let him go. His dream of a career in pro football was starting to fade. The Green Bay Packers offered him one more shot. He made the team—or so he thought—but a day later, the Packers contacted him and said they'd changed their mind. They didn't need him after all. Three strikes and Godfrey was out of the league.

"After the Packers called and let me go," he says, "I hung up the phone and fell to my knees and started to pray. I said, 'Lord, I give up. Whatever you want me to do, I'll do.' I'd never prayed like this before. Ever. Until now, I'd just mumbled prayers at Mass.

"I got up off my knees, went over to Lambeau Field (where the Packers play their games), and cleaned out my locker. The head coach, Bart Starr, saw me and called me into his office. He apologized for cutting me and said they'd changed their mind again. When he asked me to stay with the Packers, I was flabbergasted. This was the beginning of my NFL career. It was also the start of making the Catholic faith my own faith and of establishing a real relationship with God. Until that moment, I'd just been living through my parents' faith, but not anymore."

After he spent some time with the Packers, he separated his shoulder and the Packers cut him, too. This came at a very bad time, since he was engaged to be married, but as often happens, one door closed and another door opened. Once he got healthy, he was persuaded to try out for the upstart United States Football League, since by that time, the NFL was on strike. Godfrey caught on with the Michigan Panthers of the USFL and they switched him from defensive lineman to offensive lineman; it was a change that he resisted at first, but he was about to discover that he'd just found his best position on the field. When the NFL strike ended, he signed with the New York Giants and two years later he was the starting guard on the Giant team that won Super Bowl XXI in 1987. The Associated Press and UPI chose him as an All-NFC lineman and he spent four years anchoring the New York offense. After being waived in August of 1988, Godfrey played one more season with the Seattle Seahawks before retiring at the age of 31. His NFL career had been spectacular, and now his second career was about to begin.

After earning a law degree from Notre Dame in 1993, he wanted to put his faith to work. In 1992, with money given to him by the Knights of Columbus, Godfrey had made a video featuring several prominent NFL players called "Life…The Way of Champions." It took a strong pro-life stand—the first time a group of professional athletes had ever made their convictions public on this subject. The video launched Godfrey's organization, Life Athletes, which today has 300 stars from various sports, all of whom use their faith to bring a pro-life message to young audiences. Life Athletes' slogan is "Virtue, Abstinence and Respect for Life." Its pledge is this: "I will try to do what is right even if it is difficult. I promise to give myself only to that special person I marry as my partner for life. I promise to respect the lives of others, especially the unborn and the aged. I will not quit or make excuses when I fail, but I will try again."

Life Athletes speak at schools nationwide and hold summer football, soccer, basketball, and volleyball camps where kids can meet pro sports figures and talk to them about athletics and personal choices. Knights of Columbus Councils have donated funds for these camps and Order members have worked at them as volunteers in registration, food preparation, and cleanup. From the beginning, the K. of C. has been an integral part of Godfrey's spiritual and educational mission. "The Knights do whatever we ask them to do at our camps," says Godfrey, an active member of Santa Maria Council 553 in South Bend, Indiana. "They make the program go."

Godfrey's focus is reaching out to young people to join him in this work. "We show kids that what we represent isn't a bizarre way of living," he says. "A lot of accomplished, normal people have decided that our way gives them the best chance at happiness. I have kids of my own and see what kinds of things they're tempted with these days. There's a real lack of good information out there about the right choices to make and we're there to fill that need. So many of our social problems—divorce, abortion, abuse and addiction—come from the troubles created by male-female relationships. We want to do something about that."

Today, Chris and his wife Daria have six kids and they live in South Bend. Life Athletes takes up much of Chris's time: the organization produces educational videos about chastity, abstinence, and respect, and these videos are now used by Catholic schools nationwide. And while Chris is the founder and president, he has said that his former boss, Wellington Mara, who was president of the New York Giants while Chris was a player, was the inspiration for it all. It was Mara who encouraged Chris to appear in a pro-life video called "Champions for Life," and then encouraged him to create an organization that would speak for the rights of the most vulnerable in society.

Chris's mission is the same one he's been on since the day the Packers decided to give him one more chance. "We live in a sports-oriented culture," he says, "and athletes now have kids' attention. Why shouldn't we use this opportunity to help them? Why not talk to them about the most important issues in life—before they've made their decisions?"

Chris Godfrey (no. 61) playing for the New York Giants.

Paul D. Scully-Power

Early in 1984, Paul Scully-Power happened to be traveling on a flight to Washington, D.C., when he met another passenger who already knew a lot about him. That passenger, Supreme Knight Virgil Dechant, (see page 96) was aware that Scully-Power was an Australian native and a world-renowned oceanographer with decades of experience at sea. He had in fact participated in 24 scientific cruises around the globe and for thirteen of them he'd served as the chief scientist. He was an author and speaker on this subject and a qualified Navy deep-sea diver who had devoted many hours to exploring the earth's waters. At the time, he was employed by the Naval Underwater Systems Center in

New London, Connecticut, but on leave from this position because of a highly unusual mission that he and the Supreme Knight discussed during the flight. The Supreme Knight was fascinated with the adventure that lay just ahead for Scully-Power. The two men discussed something else they had in common: a deep commitment to Catholicism and the Order.

Born in Sydney, Australia, in May 1944, Scully-Power was educated at St. Pius X College, at St. Ignatius' College, and at St. John's College, University of Sydney, where he earned a degree in Applied Mathematics, with honors. He earned his Doctor of Science degree from the University of Sydney and has held the Distinguished Chair of Environmental Acoustics in the United States. His special field of expertise was called "space remote sensing" and he was credited with pioneering the science of space oceanography. This involved viewing the oceans from earth orbit, a technique particularly important during times of political or environmental crisis. He'd been an adviser to the Royal Navy during the war in the Falklands and would later be called upon by the Crown Prince of Bahrain during a major Persian Gulf oil spill.

After completing his education, Scully-Power decided to emigrate to the United States in 1977, and by 1982, he had become a U.S. citizen. Since coming to America, he has spent more than twenty years managing high technology and industry programs. These included working for the U.S. Navy, NASA, the Pentagon, and the White House, where he led a government-industry partnership for the development of advanced communications systems. He also oversaw funding for major oceanography programs at universities and research institutions on behalf of the U.S. government.

Scully-Power joined the Knights of Columbus at Seaside Council 17 in New London, Connecticut, in 1973. Nine years later, he transferred to the Father John F. Murphy Council 1943 in nearby Mystic. He and his wife, Frances, have six children, and Frances has been very active on the education committee of their parish council. When he wasn't traveling, lecturing, or diving, Scully-Power joined his wife in committee activities.

But perhaps the most exciting topic of conversation during the flight to Washington was what would soon become Scully-Power's greatest adventure as an oceanographer. He'd just been chosen as one of seven astronauts to go into space aboard the shuttle Challenger, making him the first Australian astronaut. The mission would give him the chance to view three-fourths of the world's oceans from 218 miles above the planet. He would be able to see the patterns and behaviors of global waters from a perspective never before given to someone with his education and training. As a payload specialist, he would be part of the first shuttle mission with a seven-person crew.

For the past three years, he had been involved in debriefings following each shuttle flight and had analyzed the imagery taken from the Challenger and the Gemini and Skylab programs. The data he would collect during the October 1984 mission would enhance understanding of the world's oceans. He was not only the first Australian to go into orbit but the first Knight. He told Supreme Knight Dechant during their chance meeting on the airplane that he wanted to use the flight not just for scientific research, his worldly pursuit, but to show his spiritual commitment to the Order.

Scully-Power decided to carry along an emblem of the Third Degree on a miniature flag. Before he boarded the flight, the Service Department at the Knights of Columbus headquarters in New Haven sewed the emblem to a small white silk background with gold fringe. Scully-Power kept it with him for the duration of the mission. Once he'd returned to earth, he presented the flag to the K. of C. museum, where it reminds visitors of Paul Scully-Power's devotion to both faith and science.

In 1882, Father McGivney could hardly have imagined that men would one day travel in space, or that a proud member of his beloved Knights of Columbus would be a pioneer in the early years of space exploration. Currently, Paul Scully-Power resides in Australia and is Chairman of the Australian government's International Space Advisory Group.

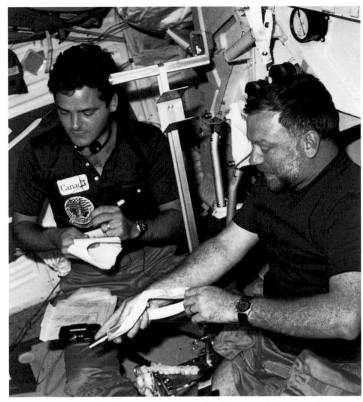

Marc Garneau (left), representing the National Research Council (NRC) of Canada, and Paul Scully-Power preparing an experiment in the mid-deck of the Challenger.

Paul Scully-Power looks at a map prior to observing and photographing an ocean feature.

Robert Sargent Shriver

R. Sargent Shriver on the cover of Time *magazine, July 5, 1963.*

John F. Kennedy embraced the idea of a Peace Corps in a speech at the University of Michigan a few weeks before the election of 1960.

Sargent Shriver, Kennedy's brother-in-law, was there that night, but he had no idea that evening how his life would soon become forever associated with one of the most popular and idealistic American initiatives of the 20th century.

The day after Kennedy was inaugurated, he telephoned Shriver and asked him to put together a presidential task force "to report how the Peace Corps should be organized and then to organize it." On February 24, Shriver delivered

the report to the White House, and on March 1, Kennedy issued an executive order "establishing a Peace Corps on a temporary pilot basis," and expressing the hope that it would be a "step in a major international effort to increase the welfare of all men." Kennedy wanted to get started immediately, and Congress could catch up later: "I recommend to the congress the establishment of a permanent Peace Corps," he wrote. With that, Sargent Shriver was off and running.

Born on November 9, 1915, he got his law degree from Yale University in 1941, and married Eunice Mary Kennedy in 1953. By the age of 44, Shriver had been a practicing attorney, an assistant editor at *Newsweek*, and president of the Chicago Board of Education. Throughout the 1960s, he'd held key advisory positions at several universities and had received seven honorary degrees. Like JFK, he was a Knight of Columbus, taking his first degree in 1956 at Chicago's Father Francis Xavier Breen.

Shriver's Peace Corps would ultimately recruit and deploy 14,500 workers to 55 countries, especially in Africa and Asia, helping to improve the health, education, and general welfare in less developed countries around the world. It was a bold idea and a resounding success. Shriver spent two and a half years building the Peace Corps into a significant and permanent force for good. He traveled constantly, and Peace Corps officials marveled at his ability to keep going without ever seeming to tire. They also learned about how seriously he took his Catholic faith. Shriver's official biographer, Scott Stossel, quotes an aide as recalling that "He kept a bible with him. He often consulted it. He got up at 5:00 A.M. to go to Mass in any city, town, or village, in any country, where there was an available church that held early mass."

Then, on November 23, 1963, President Kennedy was assassinated in Dallas. Within a few hours, Vice President Lyndon Johnson had taken the oath of office as the new president, and within two months, Johnson would tap Shriver for an even bigger task than the Peace Corps.

In January 1964, Johnson announced his War on Poverty in his first State of the Union Address to Congress. Shriver was in Pakistan at the time, and it wasn't until his return to the United States a few weeks later that he learned that Johnson had decided to put him in charge of the new effort. As had been the case with the Peace Corps, Shriver was being given an idea and the responsibility for turning it into an actual plan and piece of legislation. Pulling together a group of experts and colleagues, he soon came up with the Economic Opportunity Act. By late August, with a crucial bit of last-minute help from House Speaker and fellow Knight of Columbus John W. McCormack (see page 70), Congress had approved it and Johnson had signed it into law. In mid-October, Shriver became the first Director of the Office of Equal Opportunity (OEO), the agency assigned the task of waging the War on Poverty.

Initially, OEO was made up of two departments, Community Action and the Job Corps. But it was two other programs added several years later that had the most dramatic impact, and for which Shriver will always be remembered: Head Start and Legal Services for the Poor.

Shriver worried about the smallest humans without a voice. With legalized abortion beginning to spread in the United States in 1967, Shriver organized the first symposium on the issue. The event was held at Harvard and was sponsored by the Kennedy Foundation and Harvard Divinity School. Urging a more ethical look at biology, it was Shriver who coined the term "bioethics."

In May of 1968, the last year of the Johnson administration, Sargent Shriver became the U.S. Ambassador to France. While many wondered how Shriver would get along with the mercurial French President Charles de Gaulle, Eunice Shriver and Yvonne de Gaulle prepared the way for what turned out to be a warm relationship. Mme. de Gaulle took a strong interest in the Shrivers' work with the mentally retarded. The de Gaulles had a daughter with mental retardation who had died shortly after World War II. Eunice and Yvonne discussed the subject at length, as well as the Shrivers' plans to launch the U.S. Special Olympics program, which would stage its first event a few weeks later in Chicago in July 1968. Soon there would be a French Special Olympics to match the

program in the United States. The concept spread throughout the world. By June 1999, the Special Olympics World Summer Games had participants from 150 countries.

In 1972, Shriver was the Democratic Party's nominee for vice president, and during the campaign, reporters discovered his devout Catholicism, as Peace Corps officials had a decade earlier; throughout the campaign, he attended daily Mass wherever he went, giving quiet but unmistakable witness to the importance of Catholic faith and values in his life. He was a candidate for the Democratic presidential nomination in 1976, but Jimmy Carter proved unstoppable that year.

With children grown and government and politics now in their past, Sargent and Eunice Shriver concentrated their remarkable energy on building the Special Olympics program. Today it allows more than a million disabled athletes to participate in sporting contests on a year-round basis. In the 1980s the Knights of Columbus joined together with the Shrivers to provide both financial and volunteer support to Special Olympics activities throughout North America, and over the past three decades Knights have raised and donated $50 million for the program. The Knights and the Special Olympics were a perfect fit. Eunice Shriver summed it up best in a letter she sent to the Order in 1986.

"When a great organization like the Knights of Columbus decides to support Special Olympics," she wrote to Supreme Knight Virgil Dechant, "I know that God is looking after his children who happen to be mentally retarded."

Sargent Shriver with Supreme Knight Carl Anderson.

Virgil C. Dechant

The world of 1982 was dramatically different from the world of 1882, and the man who led the Knights of Columbus as it celebrated its first century of service transformed and modernized the Order in many ways. Virgil Dechant held the job of Supreme Knight far longer than anyone ever had—nearly 24 years—and he literally brought the organization to the doorstep of the 21st century. Along the way, he had a dramatic impact on its spiritual direction, its reach within the Catholic Church, and its financial strength.

Virgil Dechant was born in 1930. He was one of 12 children and grew up in Liebenthal, Kansas, where his father ran a general store. He studied for the priesthood at the Pontifical Josephinum Seminary in Ohio, but ultimately decided that his vocation lay elsewhere. But his experience as a seminarian gave him firsthand knowledge of their needs and concerns, and throughout his years as Supreme Knight, he devoted much thought and energy to ways of encouraging vocations.

"In my inaugural address in San Juan, Puerto Rico," he would later recall, "I referred to a survey done by Father Andrew Greeley at the National Opinion Research Center at the University of Chicago. It found that vocations come from family life. Families generate vocations." Armed with that realization, Dechant worked to develop the identity of the Knights as a family organization. From his earliest years with the Order, he demonstrated his belief that making Catholic families feel involved and welcomed should be an essential part of Knights' mission. As soon as he became Supreme Knight in January 1977, he announced plans for a new home office chapel named after the Holy Family. He also launched an enormously successful program in which local councils "adopt" one or more seminarians and receive financial help from the Supreme Council when they do. The program now provides more than $2.5 million a year to approximately 4,500 seminarians, who are supported by more than 2,500 local councils. Dechant also encouraged establishing funds that now provide scholarships for dozens of seminarians, including those pursuing advanced studies in Rome.

Among Dechant's most far-reaching initiatives was to set a goal of establishing a Knights of Columbus presence in every Catholic parish. Through much of the Order's history, councils typically put up their own buildings and often served more than one parish. Dechant shifted the emphasis to parish-based councils, meeting in church halls, and the result was tremendous growth and a much closer relationship with the parish priest. During the 32 years that Dechant served as either Supreme Secretary or Supreme Knight, he signed more than 6,000 new charters, doubling the number of councils and adding 385,000 members.

Dechant also moved to strengthen relations with the Vatican, providing funding in the early 1980s for construction of a new chapel honoring the patron saints of Europe—Saints Benedict, Cyril and Methodius—in the grottoes of St. Peter's Basilica, and the enlargement of the Chapel of Our Lady of Czestochowa. Pope John Paul II approved the architecture of the chapels at a meeting with Dechant just before the attempt on his life by a would-be assassin on May 13, 1981. "I was right there in St. Peter's Square when he was shot," Dechant recalls. "Cardinal Deskur said, 'He'll be saved. Today is the feast of Our Lady of Fatima.' And everybody relaxed. It was like a family, like nothing else I've ever seen."

The following year, 1982, was the Centennial of the founding of the Knights of Columbus, and for Dechant, it was "tremendous! My daughter got married, and our convention was two weeks later. We invited the president and the pope." President Ronald Reagan accepted the invitation, and spoke to the delegates in person, but the pope could not. "I met with John Paul II at Castel Gandolfo when he was recovering from the assassination attempt. He was still very frail." But the pope sent the Vatican Secretary of State, Cardinal Agostino Casaroli, to represent him, and history was made. "President Reagan, Cardinal Casaroli, Cardinal Pio Laghi (the Vatican's representative in the United States), and William Wilson (the presidential representative to the Vatican) all came, and in a private meeting they worked out U.S. diplomatic recognition of the Vatican. That meeting was the 'spark.' It was quite a thrill," Dechant said. Congress passed a resolution authorizing diplomatic relations the following year.

Clearly, Dechant had a significant impact on the Order's growth, its spirituality, its family orientation, encouraging vocations and its relationship with the church. But he also played a pivotal role in building the organization's financial strength.

In his home state of Kansas, he had been a very successful businessman who owned and operated a car dealership, a farm equipment firm, and his own farm. In New Haven, Connecticut, his business acumen was soon brought to bear on the Order's insurance, investments and general business affairs. Insurance agents had been part-timers, meaning that they had to take on other work as well to make ends meet. Dechant built a full-time professional agency force. "I got it

to where it was really rewarding to be an insurance agent," he said. "The insurance program gives us the muscle to answer the needs of our fellow men." During his 23 years as Supreme Knight, the amount of insurance in force grew by 1100 percent, to $40 billion.

Dechant also promoted the use of endowed funds that would support the Order's charities, rather than simply making all donations out of current budgets. The most well known of these is the Vicarius Christi Fund, established in 1981. Earnings from this $20 million fund are given to the Pope each year for his personal charities.

He had a keen appreciation for new technologies, and pushed for computerizing insurance and membership files. While he was still Supreme Secretary, he negotiated an agreement with the Vatican under which the Knights of Columbus began underwriting satellite transmission of Vatican events around the world. He also had great respect for history, and was instrumental in the founding of the Knights of Columbus Museum, which opened to the public in 2001.

Over the years, Virgil Dechant has received numerous honors from the Vatican and other religious groups. But his greatest satisfaction is knowing that he was able to do so much for the organization he has always loved. "1.7 million men are better Catholics, better husbands and fathers, and better persons because of their membership in the Knights," Dechant says. And although he retired in September 2000, after serving 24 years as Supreme Knight, what he did for the Knights and for Catholic families will long be remembered. He left a legacy of which he can be very proud.

Supreme Knight Virgil Dechant greets Pope John Paul II during a private audience, December 9, 1994.

CHAPTER SEVEN

The 1990s

Paul E. Nollette

1994-1995
INTERNATIONAL
FAMILY
OF THE
YEAR

In the mid-1990s, Paul Nollette and his wife, Jean, of Port Townsend, Washington, received a call at three in the morning. The local police department had a question. They'd just rescued a baby from a dangerous domestic abuse situation and needed a safe place for the infant. Could they drop the child off at the Nollette's home, and would Paul and Jean mind caring for the baby until other arrangements could be made? No problem, Paul said without hesitating, and soon the infant was on their doorstep. The police were very grateful and relieved because they knew the child couldn't be in a better home.

By this time, the Nollettes had already adopted three kids, to go along with four of their own, and they'd helped raise numerous foster children. But it was this ongoing desire to help small children caught in apparently hopeless conditions that caused the Washington State Council to pick the Nollettes as the state's 1995 "Family of the Year." It wasn't just home-state Knights who were impressed by their work. Later that year, for their dedication to rescuing abandoned children, Paul and Jean were named the 1995 Knights of Columbus "International Family of the Year" (see Nollette with the award, left).

The Nollettes consistently expressed their belief in building a culture of life, but didn't stop there. They participated in the March for Life at the state capital and organized transportation to the event for others. They set up a Human Life booth at county fairs, and Jean even left her job as a nurse at a public hospital when she disagreed with its position on abortion. As Paul continued working at a paper company, Jean opened an infant day care business inside their home. Soon, she and her husband began adopting children and providing foster care for some of the challenging cases in and around Port Townsend.

When babies were born prematurely, or born with brain damage, or if they'd been victims of physical abuse or prenatal drug abuse by their mothers, the Nollettes were there to take them in. The children stayed for as long as necessary, and invariably, there were always at least one or two living under the Nollette roof. The family's children learned to watch over the infants as part of their daily chores. The Nollettes taught their children that opposing abortion was not enough. It was every bit as important to help nurture babies who'd come into the world without loving parents to care for them.

For years Paul and Jean had been active in the Catholic Church, but by the early '90s, Paul was ready to do something more. He joined with two other men to form Arthur Bryant Council 10532. Paul sponsored membership drives and held open houses to bring in new members. He took on the time-consuming job of charter financial secretary, even as he and Jean continued to take in abandoned children. And although their dedication to foster care was widely known and appreciated, the Nollettes were taken aback when they learned they'd been chosen the International Family of the Year.

"We were stunned when they told us," Jean said.

"It's really kind of humbling," Paul said, "when you think about how the Knights are movers and shakers in charitable endeavors and that we were singled out from among all those people for this honor. Because the Church has been a constant for us and God has been a constant thing in our lives, we have a common thread that makes it all work for us."

Inside the Port Townsend police department and social services community, Paul and Jean have many colleagues and allies, who are extremely grateful for their efforts. One is Bill NeSmith, a social worker with the Division of Children and Family Services in Washington State.

"This family," he said, "has served as a role model to our foster children and their families. We, the staff at Children and Family Services, consider ourselves fortunate to have Jean and her family as a valuable resource in our county."

"I have known this family for twenty-two years," said local Grand Knight Robert White. "They give up new cars and things for themselves to get things for the children

they care for. When one of their foster children went to the hospital, they went with him and stayed with the baby till the baby was released…They were there to help."

The Nollettes also provide counseling for young couples ready to face the challenges of married life. And everything they do, from their involvement in the pro-life movement to caring for newborns to helping couples get off to a good start in marriage, expresses their devotion to building a society in which every child can grow up in a family setting filled with love.

And that was why, when the Port Townsend police called this couple in the middle of the night and asked for help, they already knew what the answer would be.

The Nollette family.

Beryl D. Jones

**In 1995, Beryl Jones and his wife, Janice, decided
to volunteer for the Red Cross disaster relief program**
in Oklahoma City. They'd raised seven children and Beryl
had retired from his career as a labor representative for
employees at the U.S. Postal Service. The couple had
always been socially active and they weren't at all ready
to stop. For 40 years, Beryl had been in the Knights of
Columbus and for the past decade Janice had sung in the
choir at Christ the King church. Both were busy with

church and community, but wanted to do more. Before
joining the Red Cross Quick Response Team, they had to
undergo a six-week training course to learn disaster recovery
skills, including first aid, CPR, damage assessment, and
family care. Their training ended on April 19, 1995, one of
the most infamous days in American history, and the most
notorious day ever in Oklahoma City.

That morning, after many Oklahoma City citizens had
gone to work, a huge bomb blew off the front of the Alfred
P. Murrah Federal Building, killing 168 people, including
19 children. The Joneses, who lived a number of miles from
the building, could feel the blast shake the inside of their
home, and wondered if it had been an earthquake. Within
an hour, they'd received a call from a Red Cross mobilization
unit, telling them to get ready to use their training. Beryl
and Janice were soon on their way downtown to confront
what was, at the time, the most deadly act of terrorism ever
committed on American soil. They drove to a Red Cross
warehouse to get relief supplies and set up a shelter triage
unit at St. Luke's Methodist Church. Then they went over
to what remained of the Murrah building, whose façade
had been completely blown away.

It was a scene they could never have imagined. Bits
of concrete and glass were strewn everywhere. Blood
was splattered all over the ground. The dead were being
removed, while the injured were brought into the shelter
where the Joneses and other Oklahoma City volunteers
gave them first aid. The frenetic pace of human activity
was unforgettable. What Beryl mostly remembers from that
day is people in constant motion, racing in and out of the
shelter, some carrying medical supplies and others hauling
boxes of fresh fruit donated by local grocery stores. Janice
recalls the haunted looks on the faces of those who came
to the Murrah Building looking for loved ones who'd been
lost in the blast. It was a scene beyond description—and
beyond some people's ability to cope.

Janice coped by staying busy and offering help to others. Beryl could handle what he was experiencing for two reasons: his Army service during the Korean War and his faith, which he relied upon now as never before. Yet it was still traumatic. At the end of their disaster relief site duty, both husband and wife were required to speak to a Red Cross mental health counselor. After the counselor gave Beryl and Janice a clean bill of mental health, they expressed their eagerness to continue to help, and were transferred to a family service center for bombing victims and their families. Memories of this time would never fade in intensity for the couple and neither would the stories they heard following the bombing.

That day was only the start of Beryl's volunteer efforts for the Red Cross. What he'd seen in Oklahoma City made him more committed than ever to perform this kind of service in other communities. Later, he would travel to Arizona to help fight wildfires, drive a Red Cross Emergency Response Vehicle to North Carolina in the wake of Hurricane Isabel, and both he and Janice would help with tornado recovery in the Midwest. Every time the phone rang in their home, the Joneses were prepared to pack up immediately and go wherever they were needed. In 2001, Beryl received the Red Cross Volunteer of the Year Award and the Cross of Excellence. By 2004, Beryl and Janice had been married for 48 years, and their shared Red Cross experiences had brought them even closer together.

When the Joneses weren't on a Red Cross mission, they were in Oklahoma City helping out at Christ the King Council 12669. Janice coordinated the kitchen for Christ the King's "Share and Care" dinners for Senior Citizens, while Beryl was the star of the Order's pancake breakfasts. His special batter was the talk of the parish and he was finally persuaded to reveal his secret ingredient (lemon juice), which he says makes the pancakes a lot fluffier.

Janice and Beryl attribute their ability to deal with the tragedy they've witnessed over the years to their Catholic faith and to the support they draw from the parish and the Knights. Each time they answer the call to help people caught up in a disaster, they answer God's call to serve others.

Beryl Jones has been helping disaster victims with the American Red Cross for over 10 years.

Steve Lopez

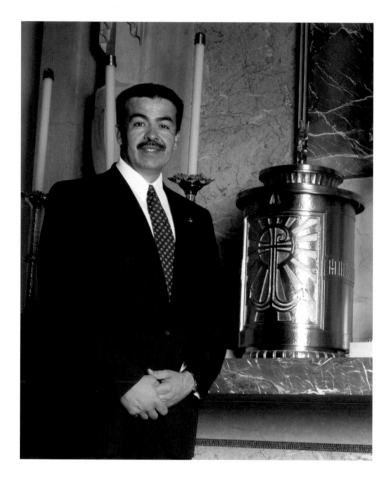

A few years ago, Steve Lopez of Idaho Falls, Idaho, was leaving Holy Rosary Church after Mass when Father Gerry Funke pulled him aside and asked why he hadn't seen him there much recently.

Taken aback by the priest's directness, Lopez fumbled for an answer. The best he could do was: "I don't make it to Mass all the time."

"Why not?" Father Funke said.

"I'm a very busy man," replied Lopez, an environmental engineer responsible for managing the nuclear waste generated at power plants around Idaho Falls.

"God is very busy, too," the priest told him, "but he takes care of you twenty-four hours a day, every day of the year."

Lopez realized he didn't have a comeback for this one. "You're right," he said.

The priest had gotten his attention and Lopez started going to church more often. One morning after Mass, Father Funke took him aside again and was just as direct this time.

"I want you to join the Knights of Columbus," he said.

"That isn't my thing," the engineer responded.

"No," the priest said, shaking his head with the same determination he'd shown earlier with Lopez. "I want you to join the Knights of Columbus so you can help other people."

The engineer started to argue but when it became clear just how serious and sincere Father Funke was, he changed his mind.

"Okay," he said, "I'll try it a few times and see if I like it."

Before long, he found himself working alongside some fellow Knights as they put a new roof on a mission church. The labor was hard, but to Lopez's surprise, he enjoyed it. He liked the fellowship, he found it rewarding to pitch in and help out, and was impressed because these Knights didn't just talk about doing things to help others: they went out and did them. What impressed him even more was that when his Council learned about a local family having financial problems after both parents had lost their jobs, the Knights decided to give them money for utility bills and other expenses until they could find work.

"What struck me," said Lopez, "was that when we were discussing this at the Council meeting, none of the Knights asked, 'Are they Catholic?' Or even, 'Are they religious?' It wasn't about what church they belonged to but about helping a family in need. That was all that mattered and that was terrific for me to see."

Each Wednesday he began serving meals at St. Mark's Soup Kitchen in Idaho Falls and volunteered to do maintenance work at a home for unwed mothers. He painted the home, landscaped it, put up a fence, and finished the basement. All this kept him busy but his real work outside of engineering came with assisting the Hispanic migrant community in southeastern Idaho.

As a volunteer with the Idaho Migrant Council, he helped people find jobs in agriculture—mainly in potato farming—and in restaurants, housekeeping positions, and in skilled trades such as metalwork, concrete work, and masonry. But he did far more than help immigrants find employment. He taught them English and stressed the importance of learning this new language, because speaking English was the key to putting down roots in America and integrating themselves into society. They couldn't take full advantage of the opportunities in front of them until they made this commitment.

"The whole idea of integration is very important to me," says the New Mexico native. "A lot of Catholic churches have Spanish Masses for Spanish-speaking people. I encourage the migrants who come here to keep their own culture but to learn English because that will lead to better jobs and better lives. There's some resistance to this, but when people see what speaking English does for them, they become believers."

In addition to all this volunteer work, Lopez finds time for evangelical work for the Church and often brings lapsed Catholics to Mass with him. Since the mid-1990s, he's committed himself to doing for others what Father Funke once did for him.

"Before I joined the Knights of Columbus," says Lopez, "my life was empty. I didn't realize that back then, but now I do. I wasn't contributing what God had in mind for me to do. That's what Father Funke saw in me and wanted me to look at. That's why he insisted that I try something new. I'm very grateful that he did."

Steve Lopez with Father Funke at a Knights of Columbus event.

John Whytal

As a boy, John Whytal used to watch his next door neighbor leave for Knights of Columbus events in his Fourth Degree regalia. "It was cool," Whytal said, "and I wanted to be a Knight, too."

Many years later, in 1990, Whytal was stationed at Scott Air Force Base, near Belleville, Illinois. There, he finally got his chance to pursue his childhood dream. He was instrumental in starting a brand new council on the base, and became a charter member of Scott Air Force Base Council 10276. "Thirty of us came in at the same time," he said. "It was really interesting, because only five or six were transfers from other councils."

Whytal adds that the Knights were "a perfect fit for the military. There's a chain of command in each one. The Air Force is headquartered in Washington, and the Knights of Columbus are headquartered in New Haven. And both organizations are full of tradition." When official travel took him away from his home council at Scott, Whytal came to appreciate the fraternal bond that greeted him wherever he went. "Whenever I could, I would go to the local Knights of Columbus council. It was always a friendly place to go."

One of the new council's first projects involved raising money for a family with a handicapped child, so that they could afford to buy a van lift. After two more years of active duty, he retired from the Air Force as a senior master sergeant and settled in Ohio near Wright-Patterson Air Force Base.

There, he joined Fairborn Council 3724, where he has raised money for scholarships to Wright State University, and other funds to buy camera equipment for the local police department, which uses it for accident investigations and domestic abuse cases. Whytal and his wife, Brenda, volunteer at St. Vincent Hotel, a homeless shelter in Dayton. Every time they hand out food, clothing, or other supplies to people who have no place to live, it teaches Whytal another lesson in humility.

"This gives me a sense of coming to the aid of others who are really down on their luck," he says. "Homeless people aren't where they are because they want to be, but because they're in a run of bad luck. You may be there yourself some day and then you're going to need people like the Knights of Columbus to give you a hand. We've been so fortunate in our lives that we feel very strongly about giving back to others. Last Christmas, we helped one lady with five kids and no husband and no job and no home. Today, she's helping out others at the St. Vincent Hotel. People can turn their lives around if they're given a chance."

Whytal also volunteers at the local Veterans Administration Hospital and the Children's Hospital. Every hour he puts in at these locations increases his appreciation for his own good health. The Knights in Ohio have lately begun "Operation Military Pride" to help out U.S. troops stationed in Afghanistan and Iraq. The Order collects and sends personal items, such as hard-to-get foods and other treats, to American military men and women in war zones.

"I was in Vietnam," Whytal says, "so I can understand what they're going through over there. When you're in a combat area, a little kindness from home goes a long way. Care packages are very meaningful, especially around the holiday season."

"Everything we do in the Order," he says, "is about following the four basic principles of the Knights of Columbus: Charity, Unity, Fraternity, and Patriotism. We can't just talk about these things. We need to put into practice what we preach, and to show people our convictions."

In addition to serving as Grand Knight of the Fairborn council, Whytal has become active in the Fourth Degree as well, ultimately becoming the top officer in Msgr. Buckley Assembly in Springfield, Ohio. And for his many achievements, he was named Knight of the Year in 2002. "In all I've done," he says, "I owe a lot to my wife because she's supported me one hundred per cent. I've put her through a tremendous amount with all these activities and I wouldn't have done nearly as much without her. She works right along with me and isn't the only woman who does this for the Knights. She isn't in this for the credit, but deserves it anyway." And the same could be said about John Whytal—he doesn't seek any praise, but he definitely deserves it for all he has done as a Knight.

John Whytal with his wife Brenda often volunteer together at Knights activities.

Judge William F. Downes

When William (Billy) Downes was a boy in Quincy, Massachusetts, he heard a lot of stories about his well-known uncle in North Carolina, Father William Patrick Ryan (see page 54). Over the decades, Father Ryan had built a stellar reputation as a priest, a Knight of Columbus, and a crusader for racial equality in the heavily segregated South during the first half of the 20th century. Because of his efforts on behalf of African Americans, the Ku Klux Klan had threatened his life, but that did not stop Father Ryan from working for civil rights. It only left him more committed to justice.

Billy understood that his uncle had gained acclaim and notoriety, but he was too young to grasp why. After graduating from North Quincy High School in 1964, the teenager went to the University of North Texas in Denton and then joined the marines. In Vietnam he served as an "artillery forward observer" who went out with the infantry and made adjustments in the artillery fire on enemy positions; he was awarded the Marine Corps' Combat Action Ribbon for his service.

One Easter Sunday, Second Lieutenant Downes was invited by Father Ryan to attend a Mass at St. Ann's parish in Fayetteville, North Carolina. The priest asked the marine to wear his uniform and carry the cross in the procession, which he did. It was a very moving occasion for the young man, and one he has never forgotten. Most worshipers in Father Ryan's congregation were black, and it was only now that Lt. Downes began to realize what his uncle had done with his life. Following the service, the marine and the priest stood side by side in the churchyard and watched a black boy and a white girl dance together.

"What do you see?" Father Ryan asked his nephew.

"Two children dancing," Lt. Downes replied. "What do you see?"

"A revolution," his uncle said. The experience of being at St. Ann's made a profound impression on the young man. In 1971, he went back to school at the University of Houston Law Center and earned his law degree in 1974. He moved to Wyoming because he loved the open landscapes of the West, and began practicing law in Casper. After working for nearly two decades as an attorney, he was appointed by President Clinton to a District Judgeship in Wyoming in 1994. If he had been sensitive to racial and civil rights issues as a lawyer, he became even more so on the bench.

"I keep a picture of Father Ryan in my office," he says. "It shows him standing in front of St. Ann's in 1940 and all of his parishioners are black. This photo always reminds me of my obligation to uphold the civil and legal rights of every American citizen."

In the early 1980s, Judge Downes joined the Knights of Columbus in Casper and soon became an active member of James E. Power Council No. 9917. He played an active role at their pancake breakfasts and other fundraisers. When he was appointed Chief United States District Judge for all of Wyoming, his schedule made washing the dishes at these breakfasts more difficult to squeeze in. But he still attends Knights functions when he can.

One year after the September 11, 2001, terrorist attacks on the United States, Judge Downes flew to Washington, D.C., for the Knights of Columbus Memorial Mass at the Basilica of the National Shrine of the Immaculate Conception. In addition to his interest in being there as a Knight, he had strong family reasons to attend. His brother, Bob, had been at the Pentagon when it was hit by a jetliner, but survived. His cousin, Ed Sullivan, an investment banker at Morgan Stanley in New York, had been in the second tower that was destroyed that morning. He too survived. As Sullivan was evacuating the building, he saw firefighters coming up the stairs to rescue those still in the tower. Most of those firemen died that day. Sullivan said that he would never forget the faces of the men he saw moving past him to get to those they were trying to save.

At the Mass, Judge Downes met Captain Alfredo Fuentes of the New York City Fire Department (see page 122). Fuentes had survived his own efforts to get others out of the towers during the attacks, but the experience had left him permanently disabled. In September 2002 at the Basilica, Captain Fuentes led the congregation in the Pledge of Allegiance, and these few words were as humbling and moving to Judge Downes as his visit to his uncle at St. Ann's Parish had been more than 30 years earlier.

"It's very good for someone like myself who works in public life to meet a real hero once in a while," he said of Fuentes. "It's inspiring to see that level of sacrifice."

Knowing Father Ryan and meeting Captain Fuentes left an indelible impression on Judge Downes.

"I try to be compassionate when dealing with all people," he says, "even those who are convicted felons. I try to remember that they are children of God even when the sentence I am imposing on them is severe. I want to respect them so this will instill in them a respect for the law. If I do that as a judge, maybe the ultimate Judge will have mercy on me in my final judgment."

The photograph that hangs in the office of Judge William Downes. Father William Patrick Ryan (back row, seventh from left) stands with the parishioners of St. Ann's Church in Fayetteville, North Carolina, 1940.

Donald D. Lederhos

For more than four years, Donald Lederhos studied for the priesthood at Washington's Gonzaga University seminary. He wanted to lead a life of service to his faith, his Church and his community, but ultimately he decided that his vocation was elsewhere. He married, and he and his wife, Karen, had four children.

In the 1970s, they started a home for mentally disabled children in Spokane. Then, in 1977, the Lederhos family moved up to Anchorage, Alaska, where Don opened Raven Electric Inc. in 1978. The company provides electrical services to businesses and residences throughout the state. He joined Habitat for Humanity, and began using his far-above-average handyman skills to help the group provide housing for people who couldn't afford it. In addition to wiring homes for Habitat for Humanity, he also did electrical work for local Catholic parishes at cost.

He bought a house in Anchorage and converted it into a Catholic youth recreational center and an office for himself. He wanted to work inside the center, located right next to his parish, so he could supervise the young people while running his business. He rewired the building and refurbished it, putting in a furnace and phone lines. He painted the walls and dug a well. The center offered after-school and evening activities, games, and a place for meetings and sleepovers. With the center up and running, Don was able to realize his goal of being an involved Catholic layman, even as he continued to manage Raven Electric. As many as 60 youngsters use the center at any one time, and things can be hectic, but it's the kind of challenge Lederhos enjoys.

"There are days," he says, "when I'm not totally focused on business in my office, but that's all right, because I love being able to help young people."

In the late 1990s, he joined the Knights of Columbus and began doing even more volunteer work around Anchorage—in the Toys for Tots program, in Bowling for Kids, in sponsoring youth baseball and hockey leagues, and by supporting the Boys and Girls Clubs of Alaska. He raised money for the American Lung Association and the Abused Women's Aid in Crisis. He committed himself to giving an annual contribution of $25,000 a year for Catholic youth programs, making him the area's single largest local donor to Catholic social services.

"After I opened my business and became successful at it," he says, "I decided that I didn't need all the money I was making and could use it to help others, especially kids. That's what I've been doing ever since."

He provided free electrical wiring and smoke detectors for Anchorage's House of Discernment, where young men come to explore the possibility of a priestly vocation, a process that Lederhos knows well.

In helping to encourage young men to consider vocations, Lederhos is continuing a long tradition of the Knights of Columbus. The Knights provide both need-based and merit-based scholarships for seminarians through the Father Michael J. McGivney scholarship fund and the Bishop Thomas V. Daily scholarship fund. Local councils that support individual seminarians receive encouragement in the form of partial rebates of their donations through the RSVP program. And there's also a Knights of Columbus assistance program for priests who receive continuing education abroad. In 2003 alone, the Knights gave more than $6.3 million dollars to support seminarians, $1.8 million to support vocations, and $1.6 million to various seminaries. Local councils and individual Knights are an important part of providing support to seminarians, and many, like Lederhos, do an exemplary job.

In 2001, Lederhos served as both Vocations Chairman and Deputy Grand Knight of St. Patrick Council 11745. In 2002 and 2003, he served as the Council's Grand Knight, and took on the task of membership chairman, too.

This man of inexhaustible energy sees the Knights of Columbus as the place to be for Catholic men who share his desire to give support to their church and to the Anchorage community.

"Last year," he says, "I brought in more Knights to our Council than anyone else in the state. I brought in seventeen or eighteen new members. It wasn't hard to do. I'd ask men why they hadn't joined the Knights of Columbus and they'd usually say the same thing—'because nobody has asked me.' I'd ask them right then and they'd say yes. They were ready to get involved and just looking for the right opportunity. It was really that simple."

Donald Lederhos with Archbishop Hurley as he raises money for a Knights of Columbus fundraiser.

Raymond L. Flynn

The son of a longshoreman and a cleaning woman, Ray Flynn rose from poverty to become one of America's 20th-century statesmen. Born on July 22, 1939, the South Boston native was a star athlete in high school and then grabbed headlines in college as an Academic All-American on the Providence College Friars basketball team. He was the Most Valuable Player at the 1963 National Invitational Tournament in New York City and was drafted to play in the National Basketball Association by the Syracuse Nationals (which later became the Philadelphia 76ers). Although he never became a star in the NBA, he found success in the college coaching ranks, becoming a baseball and basketball coach at Stonehill College, a Catholic college located in North Easton, Massachusetts. He also earned a Master's Degree in Education from Harvard.

But when Flynn was elected to the City Council in Boston in 1977, he started making news of a different kind.

This Knight had always had strong opinions about what it meant to be a Catholic and a Democrat—a Democrat with deep pro-life convictions—and it had never been his style to hide his beliefs. He'd become a Knight in the 1960s, joining Boston's Pere Marquette Council 271. The more prominent he became, the more he had to say about where politics and faith intersected.

In 1978, the Massachusetts legislature enacted a statute known as the Doyle-Flynn Law, over the veto of Governor Michael Dukakis. Under this statute, Massachusetts would not pay for most abortions. Flynn also backed legislation requiring parental notification and consent for abortions performed on minors. In 1977, he made no secret of his religious background when he publicly condemned the movie "Nasty Habits," which satirized the Church in general and, as Flynn put it, "all Catholics in particular."

In 1984 he became the mayor of Boston. He was reelected twice, the last time with 75% of the votes, the biggest majority ever in a Boston mayoral race. If he was outspoken on maintaining traditional values, Flynn was also a champion for the downtrodden and for victims of discrimination. Flynn worked tirelessly to pass the Stuart B. McKinney Homeless Assistance Act of 1987 and proposed a National Community Housing Partnership to commit the United States to building affordable housing for working Americans. In 1991, Flynn became president of the U.S. Conference of Mayors and sought to highlight the issues of homelessness and urban renewal. While mayor and afterwards, he made a point of spending time in Boston's poorer neighborhoods, where he laced up his tennis shoes and played pickup basketball games with the locals. He liked the rough-and-tumble exchange of street ball as much as he enjoyed the give-and-take of politics.

In 1993, President Clinton appointed him U.S. Ambassador to the Holy See, a position Flynn held till 1997. Flynn chose Gate of Heaven Church in South Boston, the church where he was baptized, and where he had attended for many years, to make his acceptance speech; the occasion was filled with both his personal history and emotion. When Flynn was a boy, his mother would come home from cleaning floors all day and go drop a dollar in the collection basket at Gate of Heaven. The significance of her sacrifices and her steadfast faith was not lost on the ex-mayor.

Filled with appreciation, he talked of his mother and said, "Here is her son, nominated to represent the United States at the Vatican…I never thought this was possible."

Flynn also wrote to Supreme Knight Virgil Dechant about how much it meant to him to be a Knight. "Being a member of the Knights of Columbus is a source of great pride to me. Thanks for all your strong leadership," he wrote.

A strong advocate of programs for the poor, Flynn acknowledged that the welfare system needed revamping.

But that, he said, did not justify removing all government aid to those who were trying to help themselves.

"I believe," he said, "as I think Pope John Paul II does, that in the defense of life—born and unborn—material support is no vice, and more such support is better than less because it would help build better families and a stronger country."

In 2004, Flynn helped found and became national chairman of Catholic Citizenship, an organization dedicated to taking his message of voting in a way consistent with Catholic teaching to a national audience. Writing on the subject of conscientious voting in *Columbia* Magazine just before the 2004 election, Flynn said: "Do not think of yourself as a Democrat or a Republican, a liberal or a conservative. Think of yourself instead as a proud, loyal, and faithful pro-life Catholic. Remember God, country and family. That is what the Knights of Columbus has stood for since our founding."

Ray Flynn and Pope John Paul II.

Father Ronald P. Pytel

On October 5, 1995, Father Ronald Pytel of Baltimore's Holy Rosary Parish fell to the floor of his church, unable to move. Several months earlier, he'd been diagnosed with a congenital heart defect caused by massive calcium buildups, and had undergone surgery to have a mechanical aortic valve inserted into his chest. During the operation, doctors found such extensive damage to Father Pytel's heart that they suggested the 48-year-old take early retirement, and were concerned that he would face an early death. He would certainly, in the opinion of the medical world, never be able to return to his regular pastoral duties. The priest, a Knight of Columbus in Father Burggraff Council 6021, had carefully considered this prognosis but had not been willing to accept it as the final word.

On that October 5, Father Pytel and some friends had gathered at Holy Rosary Parish for a full day of prayer for his healing. For 12 hours, they prayed and venerated a relic of a Polish nun, Sister Faustina Kowalska. It was the anniversary of her death in 1938, and while praying, they asked her to intercede on Father Pytel's behalf. Near the end of the day he collapsed to the floor and for 15 minutes he lay paralyzed but conscious, as a strange warmth passed through the length of his body. It was unlike anything he'd ever felt and he wondered if it was the presence of the nun herself.

She was born Helen Kowalska on August 25, 1905, one of ten children of an impoverished peasant family in central Poland. She had only three years of schooling, and worked as a domestic, but she knew from childhood that she was called to be a nun. She was rejected by several convents, but finally in August 1925, when she was 20, she entered the Warsaw convent of the Congregation of the Sisters of Our Lady of Mercy. She took the name Sister Maria Faustina of the Most Blessed Sacrament. Thirteen years later, at age 33, she would die of tuberculosis, but during her final years, despite being nearly illiterate, she was able to keep a diary of her mystical visions of Christ and of his revelations to her. In one vision, Jesus instructed her to have a picture of him painted, with the inscription "Jesus I trust in You." This event would later become very important to Father Pytel

In February of 1931, Christ had told Sister Faustina to make a painting of his image as he'd appeared in the vision. The painting, so well known today, was completed in oils by the artist Eugeniusz Kazimirowski in June 1934. On September 13, 1935, Christ directed her to spread his message of mercy and dictated to her a new form of devotion known as the Divine Mercy. The following day, Christ taught her to pray the chaplet, which she would describe as the "prayer that serves to appease the wrath of God."

Following her death on October 5, 1938, her diary was discovered, but the Vatican banned its publication until 1978. That year the Archbishop of Krakow, Karol Wojtyla, who six months later would be elected Pope John Paul II, became personally interested in Sister Faustina. He worked to have the ban retracted and her reputation restored, which was done. In 1981 Sister Faustina was credited with interceding and healing Maureen Digan of Lee, Massachusetts, of a painful disease called lymphedema. Twelve years later, the recognition of this healing as a miracle led to her beatification.

Father Pytel, the grandson of Polish immigrants, had closely studied the nun's history and in October 1995, he called upon her to help him. He also drew upon the depths of his faith. What science could not accomplish, perhaps prayer could. After lying unmoving for 15 minutes and feeling that warmth course through him, the priest was able to stand and return to a functional state. He appeared the same, but something had changed. The following month he visited the hospital for a checkup and Dr. Nicholas J. Fortuin, a world-renowned cardiologist at Baltimore's Johns Hopkins University, was startled by what he saw. The calcium buildups that had caused Father Pytel's heart defects were gone. The priest was cured. Father Pytel contacted Father Seraphim Michalenko of Stockbridge, Massachusetts, the North American representative for furthering the cause of Sister Faustina's canonization.

In November and December 1999, medical and theological experts met to look at the evidence. The medical team proclaimed their belief that the healing of Father Pytel's heart could not be explained by science. The theological team formally attributed it to the intercession of Sister Faustina. On December 20, 1999, a decree establishing this as a miracle was read in the presence of Pope John Paul II. The Holy Father named the Polish nun the first saint of the new millennium and called her a "gift of God for our time." The historical period in which Christ had appeared to her, the Pope noted, occurred between the two World Wars.

"Those who remember, who were witnesses and participants in the events of those years and the horrible suffering of millions of people," the Holy Father said, "know how necessary the message of mercy was."

On April 30, 2000, as Rome was filled with blooming flowers and budding trees, the Pope celebrated the canonization Mass in front of more than 300,000 people in St. Peter's Square. John Paul II declared to the huge audience that the Sunday after Easter would forever after be known as "Divine Mercy Sunday."

"With this act," the Holy Father said in Polish, "I intend to transmit today this message to the new millennium. The people of today must be inspired by this love in order to face the crisis of meaning, the challenges of diverse needs, above all the need to safeguard the dignity of each human person."

The celebration of Sister Faustina would touch millions, but no one more directly than Father Pytel. Through her intercession, God had given him good health and more years to live, while his prayers had set in motion the events leading to her canonization. Although he died of cancer he never doubted that his faith had been rewarded. He was always grateful for that gift of extra time, and as he explained it, "I know in my heart that Faustina put in a word with Jesus, and his heart touched mine."

Father Pytel after the canonization Mass of Sister Faustina by Pope John Paul II, April 30, 2000.

CHAPTER EIGHT

The 2000s

Lieutenant Daniel O'Callaghan

As a boy growing up on Long Island, New York, Danny O'Callaghan was afraid of heights. Maybe that's why it took him a while to find his true calling. He'd come from a long line of police officers and for the first three years of his career, he tried to follow their path, but although he shared their desire to serve others, he eventually decided that he would be happier as a New York City fireman. As soon as he made the switch, everything fell into place.

He loved driving to the firehouse each morning, loved the men he saw there every day, and loved the job itself. He was like a kid who'd found the magical place he'd always wanted to be. Between emergencies, he entertained the guys by telling jokes and romping around the firehouse. He didn't do this just to amuse his fellow workers but tohelp them let go of the fear and tension that comes with being in a line of work where they faced one crisis after another. He used humor to balance out the dark side of firefighting and to remind them that somebody cared about them enough to do whatever it took to make them momentarily forget the dangers of their jobs—and just laugh.

Lt. O'Callaghan always prepared himself for the worst disasters. No matter the weather, he walked around Ladder Company 4 in Midtown Manhattan in thick black bunker pants. When the bell rang, he didn't have to change clothes the way some other firefighters did. He was instantly ready to jump on the fire engine and head into another life-and-death situation. Once he reached the scene of a fire, his old fear of heights vanished. When somebody else's life was on the line, his trepidation about climbing ladders or up trees or standing on top of buildings disappeared. This 42-year-old Knight was not merely the jokester at Ladder 4, but the leader of his firehouse by attitude and example. Everyone knew one thing above all about Danny O'Callaghan: he would do whatever it took to help whomever he could.

On the morning of September 11, 2001, he left for work from Smithtown, Long Island, after distributing a few yellow Post-it® notes around the house for his wife, Rhonda, and their two small children. His daughter, Rhiannon Rose, was six, and his son, Connor Daniel, was 17 months. He kept pictures of them taped up at his space in the firehouse. Before going to the fire station each morning, he left notes that Rhonda would find and read to herself and the kids. Sometimes, the Post-its just had smiling faces on them or said, "I miss you" or "I love you." Rhonda liked to read the messages a couple of times a day and send her husband silent thoughts about his safety.

Danny O', as they called him at Ladder 4, always went to work with a battered prayer card stapled to a book of matches inside his jacket pocket. He would glance at it when the bell rang and it was time to answer another call. The card represented his connection to his faith, but for some reason he left it behind in Smithtown on this particular day. His wife would later it find it in their house, along with some other personal effects.

After two jetliners smashed into the World Trade Center towers that morning, Ladder 4 was called in to help put out fires, rescue the wounded, and manage the worst crisis the New York City Fire Department had ever seen. When he arrived at the horrendous scene, Danny O' did what he always did: he didn't ask questions or hesitate but rushed into the buildings to save as many lives as he could. But this disaster was larger than any he or his supervising officers had ever imagined. By the time Danny got inside and began doing his job, the buildings were already unsteady and starting to topple. He went in anyway, committed to saving whomever he could. But there was nobody who could rescue Lt. O'Callaghan. Along with so many of his brothers that day, he was crushed to death in the rubble as the building fell—killed doing the job he most wanted to do and what he believed was the very best thing he could do for his fellow New Yorkers. Sadly, he had just been promoted the day before; had he lived, he would have been a captain.

Just a few months earlier, he'd joined the Knights of Columbus after his brother Timothy had convinced him that it was an organization where he belonged. He was just getting started in the Order when he sacrificed his life for others on September 11. A faithful Knight and a man who used prayer every day in his work, the rosary beads Danny carried with him everywhere were found in the wreckage at the World Trade Center. They were used to help identify his remains.

If the men at Ladder 4 ever needed comic relief to help them cope with their losses, the time was now, but the guy who'd made everyone howl with laughter was gone. They all had memories of his pranks and jokes, and all were struck by the enormous silence his death had left behind. It would be a long time before anyone at Ladder 4 could make them laugh like that again.

On Long Island, he was sorely missed in Smithtown, and so were his morning Post-its. His small drawings and handwritten messages had connected him each day to the people he loved the most, until he came back home for the night. They could no more be replaced than he could. But to his family, as to all New Yorkers, Danny O' was a hero. His name and the names of 14 other firefighters who lost their lives that day were engraved on a black granite fountain, in a park across from the firehouse where they used to work. Firefighters continue to come by, to remember them and say a prayer. The Knights too put up a memorial exhibit at their museum. Among the items on display were the fire captain's hat that Danny had never gotten to wear.

In the end, he embodied the spirit described in the Gospel of John: "Greater love has no man than this, that a man lay down his life for his friends."

The Twin Towers burning just before their collapse, on September 11, 2001.

Captain Alfredo N. Fuentes

Many of us have wondered what we would do if confronted with almost certain death—and had the time to think about what was coming. On September 11, 2001, Alfredo (Al) Fuentes, a captain in the New York City Fire Department, got that opportunity and turned to the greatest source of comfort and hope he'd ever known. That morning he was acting battalion chief for his division when the World Trade Center towers were struck by two hijacked commercial jets. His job was to lead fireboat rescue teams from the Brooklyn Naval Yard to Lower Manhattan and ferry survivors to hospitals. He went about this relentlessly,

doing all he could do to find the wounded and get them to a fireboat as quickly as possible. Before the south tower came down, he had assisted in evacuating seven firefighters and other personnel from the wreckage and moved them to safety. Then he went to work in the north tower, looking for more people to rescue. Suddenly, the north tower began crumbling all around him.

Before he could attempt to get out of the way, a steel girder landed on Fuentes' upper body, pinning him to the ground. The weight of the metal fractured his skull and smashed his left hand, snapping the bones in two of his fingers. The girder broke nine of his ribs and collapsed his lung. He was in excruciating pain and was in and out of consciousness for the next 45 minutes. However, he was able to maintain radio contact with other rescuers and guide them to where he lay trapped. During that time, he also said the Hail Mary over and over again, said it from the depths of his being and then said it some more. In the face of death, that prayer was his most faithful companion. As the pain was about to overwhelm him, the rescuers finally arrived, removed the girder, and rushed him to a hospital.

Fuentes' injuries were severe—the NYC Fire Department ruled him permanently and totally disabled—and for the next four months, he needed constant attention. His wife, Eileen, left her job to be with him every day and slept beside him on a cot at the hospital. His son, Matthew, took care of the two younger children at home. His fellow Knights at George W. Hudson Council 3701 in Woodside, New York, regularly visited Fuentes in the hospital, which reminded him of why he'd spent 20 years in the Order and of how many men were now praying for him. His body had been crushed, but his faith in his homeland and Church was stronger than ever.

"What America has done and how we rallied for our fellow human beings after September 11," he said, "is what the Knights have been doing all along. I think that's what their role is—to teach everybody about love of country and their commitment to humanity. It's ironic how in the Knights we call each other brothers and in the fire department we call each other brothers—that's so wonderful, it almost brings me to tears." Fuentes gave a detailed account of his ordeal and recovery in a book entitled *American by Choice*.

On the first anniversary of the World Trade Center attacks, the Knights of Columbus held a Mass and patriotic program at the Basilica of the National Shrine of the Immaculate Conception in Washington, D.C. In full regalia, Fourth Degree Knights walked two by two up the stairs and into the nation's patronal shrine, passing beneath a 30-by-50-foot American flag and the 329-foot Knights' Tower. Supreme Knight Carl Anderson and Bishop Thomas V. Daily of Brooklyn led a candle-lighting ceremony, using a tiny oil lamp to start the ritual. It was the same lamp the Pope had employed eight months earlier at a prayer meeting for 200 leaders of world religions in Assisi, Italy. While Bishop Daily recited the same prayer for peace that the Pope had offered at Assisi, Fourth Degree Knights lit candles throughout the Basilica, the flames standing as a sign of renewal and hope for the future.

Despite his disability and the ongoing pain, Alfredo Fuentes had made the trip to Washington and was now called upon to say the Pledge of Allegiance. He'd been asked to appear at numerous events on this tragic anniversary and turned all of them down, except this one. Because of his longstanding connection to the Knights and their support for him after his injuries, he'd chosen to attend this event over all others.

"It's an honor to be involved in this day and to lead the pledge," he told the worshipers before delivering the words that were familiar to everyone present. No one hearing the voice of this disabled man was unmoved and most were left in tears.

He told the assembled worshipers that he'd marked this anniversary by paying attention to those whose losses were worse than his own.

"My wife and I this morning called all the widows of the firefighters we knew," he said on September 11, 2002. He paused and added, "That's a lot of people."

Al Fuentes had seen many changes in his life since he came to America from Ecuador as a child. He joined the Knights in 1973, as a member of George W. Hudson Council, and his dedication to the Knights was equaled by his dedication to the New York Fire Department. Both organizations shaped his adult life. He is now retired from the fire department and when not doing speaking engagements or raising money for charity, he works as a consultant: he is the founder of the Patriot Group, a not-for-profit organization that trains and assists first responders.

Captain Alfredo Fuentes addressing college leaders of the Knights of Columbus in 2004.

Vincent P. Valerio

Vincent "Vinnie" Valerio had been a corrections officer before going to work for the Knights of Columbus as a field agent in April 2001. He'd been on the job only five months on September 11, 2001. That same day, in the wake of the attacks that killed more than 3,000 people, the Order pledged a million dollars to the families of the firefighters, police officers, and rescue personnel who had given their lives in an attempt to save others. Now it was up to Valerio and other field agents to locate the family members, establish contact with them, and give them $3,000 checks from the Knights' "Heroes Fund." By September 12, Vincent had begun carrying out a mission unlike anything he'd ever done or imagined doing.

The most difficult part at first was locating the victims' relatives. While conducting his search, he visited firehouses and police stations, went to funerals and wakes throughout the metropolitan area, and scoured the papers for clues. Once he'd found addresses for survivors, he knocked on their doors, explaining why he was there as gently as he could. Many people didn't want to speak to him, no matter what he had to say or offer. When another field agent went to a victim's residence, a sign on the front door read, "Come home soon, Daddy." Such experiences were common.

Some of the victims' next of kin were angry or hostile, but Vincent persisted and gradually made progress. He had one thing going for him that many others didn't. His wife, Patricia, worked at Staten Island's Holy Child Roman Catholic Church, and several of the September 11 victims had ties there. That helped, and so did the legwork he did around the clock. He refused to stop when the job seemed completely overwhelming. Over the first few weeks, he was able to get many victims' widows to sign the affidavits needed to establish their personal connection to those who'd died. Vincent faxed the affidavits to Knights of Columbus headquarters in New Haven and the following day, he was usually handing out the money the Knights had marked for this purpose.

The Order had streamlined the process, and so in most cases, the first money families received after the tragedy came from the Knights of Columbus. By December 1, 2001, the organization had given checks totaling $1.25 million to 417 families of the fallen. The checks were used for everything from buying groceries to paying a mortgage. When the fund was closed on July 15, 2002, each of the assisted families, which had grown to 419, were sent a further gift of $542.

In early 2002, the Order held a nationwide "Blue Mass." Named in honor of the navy blue color of police and firefighter uniforms, it provided a show of solidarity with uniformed service personnel across the country. Led by Supreme Knight Carl Anderson at St. Mary's Church in

New Haven, the special Mass became an annual event and provided an opportunity to highlight two of the Knights of Columbus ideals: Fraternity and Charity. Supreme Knight Anderson also encouraged each Council to offer a "Firefighter of the Year" award and a "Police Officer of the Year" citation to a local member.

In the aftermath of September 11, no one in the Knights did more for the surviving victims than Vincent Valerio. His background was similar to many of those who'd died trying to rescue people at the World Trade Center. This helped him get close to their families and was a major reason he was able to reach more families than any other agent. He personally handed out more than 70 checks before the program ended and he was able to return to his job of protecting families' futures by providing them with life insurance.

Like many others who'd been through the emotionally exhausting work that followed September 11, Vincent had trouble quickly transitioning back to his former employment. It had taken all his inner resources to deal with what he'd been asked to do for others who'd lost a loved one. He was particularly moved by a New York City Port Authority police officer's widow who'd been left with a ten-month-old baby.

She was shattered and had no idea where to turn after losing her husband. Vincent spent hours with her, comforting her and offering advice, and promising to return soon with a check. He did the same thing for most of the other grieving families. He gave them much more than a check; he gave them a person to talk to and a shoulder to cry on. He gave them someone who really cared about their loss and their struggles. Shortly thereafter, he was diagnosed with cancer. He began chemotherapy treatments and many people whose lives he touched have prayed for his recovery.

On December 4, 2001, Supreme Knight Carl Anderson signed a resolution honoring Vincent and the other agents who had accomplished so much with the Heroes Fund during the preceding months. The agents' actions, Anderson said, exemplified the "spiritual and corporal works of mercy" and were "expressive of the sympathy felt by our Order for those who suffered such an egregious loss." And he especially took note of the "personal emotional toll" felt by the agents who delivered the checks. Vincent Valerio and his fellow agents devoted countless hours to helping rebuild broken lives, and carried a message of faith and hope to the families of hundreds of the fallen heroes of 9/11.

Heroes of 9/11 are honored at a display at the Knights of Columbus museum in New Haven, Connecticut. The helmet on the right belonged to a Knight who died at the World Trade Center that day.

Paul Marretti

Paul Marretti is a young man who has had mental disabilities since childhood. He lives in Richmond, Virginia, and, as he explained to delegates to the 2003 Knights of Columbus Supreme Convention in Washington, D.C., "I am one example of more than one million athletes around the world who benefit from your work and generosity."

Ever since Sargent (see page 94) and Eunice Shriver sponsored the very first Special Olympics event in Chicago in 1968, the Knights of Columbus have provided both financial support and manpower for Special Olympics, which honors and celebrates the lives of persons with mental disabilities. Its motto is, "Let me win. But if I cannot win, let me be brave in the attempt." These Games, which offer a year-round program of sports training and athletic competition for children and adults with these disabilities, are all about a wonderful kind of bravery. They provide opportunities for developing physical fitness, for sharing skills with friends and families, for being active members of the community, and for getting off the sidelines and engaging with others. They are designed to show the athletes that they can do far more than they dreamed possible. Every once in a while, a Special Olympian comes along with an unshakable desire not just to compete but to help those like himself. This individual is an example of hope for others and takes on the mission of bringing the Games to disabled people everywhere.

As a youngster, Paul Marretti began his sports career by playing softball, basketball, tennis, golf, and soccer, in addition to Alpine skiing, bowling, and aquatics. While he loved taking part in these activities, he was even more committed to getting other kids onto the fields or the courts or the slopes. If he could do all these things and draw so much joy from competing, he knew others could as well. In 1995, he convinced a local baseball league to sponsor a softball event in Richmond's new ballpark to benefit the Special Olympics. To his surprise and everyone else's, the event was a huge success, raising tens of thousands of dollars that helped launch and sustain many of the area's Special Olympic programs.

With this funding in place, Paul got involved in Special Olympics as a participant, winning three medals at the 2001 Special Olympics Virginia Summer Games. His reputation as an athlete was spreading and so was his work as an ambassador for the Games. In 2002, he became a member of the Knights of Columbus at Bishop Ireton Council 6189 in Richmond, and was soon speaking to groups about the benefits of the Games. Every two years, a dozen athletes are selected to represent the Special Olympics as Global Messengers, and in 2002, Paul won this distinction. As the "Sargent Shriver International Global Messenger," Paul was chosen to spread the vision of the Special Olympics across the United States and beyond.

When at home in Richmond, he stayed busy working at a Kroger grocery store and quietly living by himself, but on the road he was a featured public speaker—sharing his experience with disabled athletes everywhere and telling them how the Games could offer them acceptance, dignity, and the chance to excel at sports. He talked about how the Special Olympics had changed his view of himself, and how it could open doors for others. Paul's emphasis was not just on competition but on promoting leadership among the disabled in Special Olympic programs, because this would keep them connected to the Games long after they'd stopped competing. Paul recruited other Special Olympic athletes to serve as Board Members for their regions and now serves on the Special Olympics Virginia Board of Directors.

As a Global Messenger, he was no longer just a local speaker, but traveled around the country and flew to Dublin, Ireland, to carry his message of active involvement for disabled athletes. At Dublin's 2003 Special Olympics World Summer Games, Paul addressed more than 75,000 people at the opening ceremony and told them his story of hope and helping others. He also met many celebrities, including Muhammad Ali, Bon Jovi, Dylan McDermott, and Nelson Mandela, all of whom were celebrating the international success of the Special Olympics. The Knights had donated $1 million to cover the travel expenses of the teams from the United States, Canada, and Mexico.

In August 2003, Paul attended the Knights of Columbus 121st Annual Supreme Council meeting in Washington, D.C., and was a featured speaker for the 2,500 people who came to the States Dinner. He laid out in detail his work with the Games and expressed his appreciation for the ongoing legwork and monetary support the Knights are giving to this cause.

"It's always nice to be among friends who are so involved in two organizations which have so dramatically changed my life, Special Olympics and Knights of Columbus," he began. "Without the Knights of Columbus, Special Olympics athletes like me simply would not have the opportunities we do.

"Long before I was chosen as a Global Messenger, Special Olympics helped me by allowing me to play sports just like everyone else, all of you here in this room, by allowing me to develop physically, socially and emotionally just like everyone else and by allowing me to be an active, contributing part of my community just like everyone else.

"On behalf of Special Olympic athletes everywhere, I say as sincerely as I can, thank you. But I'm not finished yet. You add value to all our lives. Hopefully along the way we add value to your lives, too."

Paul's energy and enthusiasm are impossible to ignore. He can be so persuasive that in April of 2005, he was part of a 20 person delegation that went to Washington, D.C., to lobby congress for more funding for programs that benefit those with mental disabilities. Anyone who has seen him compete or heard him speak can understand why the Knights have chosen to back Special Olympics, and to honor Paul Marretti. The reason is very simple: the Games make everybody connected with them a better person.

Paul Marretti speaks at the 2003 Supreme Convention of the Knights of Columbus.

Kevin Lopresti

Every October Kevin Lopresti, the chief electrical operations engineer with the Canadian Pacific Railway, begins preparations for a special job. For the next two months he works around the clock, getting ready to spread the Christmas spirit literally from one end of Canada to the other. His work at this time of year becomes an expression of his faith, his celebration of the holiday season, and his service as a Knight of Columbus. For these 60 days, he also puts in a lot of overtime.

In the mid-1990s, Canadian Pacific executives came to him with an unusual request. They wanted Lopresti to oversee putting together an eight-car, 1,000-foot, festively decorated train that would travel across western Canada each December, collecting food at each stop. The food would then be handed out to the poor in each of the 30 or so towns along the route. Lopresti, a husband, father, and Knight of Columbus at Archbishop Monahan Council

4878 located at St. Cecilia's Parish in Calgary, undertook the challenge with enthusiasm and energy.

That first October, he designed the train, selecting huge wreaths for the locomotive, Christmas trees for the cars, and roughly 8,500 Christmas lights that gave the train a holiday glow. Initially, the lights were all white, but after a while he began using blue, red, gold, yellow, and green bulbs. He picked out the stops the train would make on its 3,000-mile run and coordinated maintenance, food collection, and distribution on a trip that ended in Vancouver. He made sure there were enough ladders and forklifts and workers in case repairs had to be made in the middle of the night. The media were amazed and impressed by Lopresti's efforts. In December 1999, as reporters watched the Holiday Train rolling into each station, a journalist from Calgary punned that "Rudolph isn't here, but there's definitely a red-nosed train, dear." The huge locomotive that he observed was certainly larger than a sleigh—it "packed the mechanical power of 4,300 horses" and arrived illuminated with more than 5,000 lights, representing each kilometer of the trip across Canada. But more important than its size was how it was bringing hope to those in need during the holiday season, thanks in large part to dedicated volunteers and inspired by Kevin Lopresti.

"I've been picking out lightbulbs and laying down carpet at three in the morning," Lopresti says. "Fifteen-hour days and long nights are normal on this job."

The journey starts in late November and runs through the first two weeks of December. Of course, the most inter-esting part is what unexpectedly happens when taking a train across Canada in wintertime. A few years ago, the locomotive was making its way through a tunnel at Rogers Pass in the Rocky Mountains of British Columbia. The heat from the train caused the hoar frost inside the tunnel to melt and drop from the ceiling, knocking out the colored lights on the cars—lots of them. By the time the train had come to a halt and the damage could be assessed, 3,000 bulbs needed replacement. That's when it pays to have the nation's leading railway electrical engineer on board.

The holiday trip across the Rockies became so successful that in 2001, the Canadian Pacific decided to ask him to put together another train to make an eastern swing and distribute more food to the needy. This one would begin its journey in New York State and travel north to Montreal and Toronto, for a total of around 2,500 miles. It would hold a few less cars and lights than the western train but follow the same basic strategy, carrying singers and other entertainers who drew crowds at each stop. Within a year or two, the eastern swing had become just as popular as the western one and both were bringing in tens of thousands of dollars in cash and food.

Lopresti no longer makes the entire trip on either train but is present during the first five or six hundred miles to make sure everything is functioning properly. If hoar frost isn't breaking lights by the thousands in Rogers Pass, then falling trees and branches along the route often keep the crew busy all day and deep into the night.

"A lot of repair work goes into keeping a train like this running in the winter," Lopresti says. "We've gone through snowstorms and freezing rain and every other kind of weather you can imagine, but we've never been stopped. We've seen it thirty-five to forty below outside but we've managed to keep everything running. I've spent many nights fixing the furnaces and generators."

He originally joined the Knights of Columbus to help serve his community, but now he's helping people all across Canada. The Christmas trains have become an expression of his faith in action. For Lopresti, his holiday job and the Order's mission are one.

"Working with all the lights on the train is very labor-intensive," he says, "but when we pull into a town and see the people coming toward us holding out bags of groceries, it really affects you. When you watch the food being given to those who need it the most you understand why we're making all this effort. That's when you know that all the hours and effort were worth it."

Santa waves from the Holiday Train that Lopresti puts together every year.

Daniel D. Sieve

Nationwide, the Knights have 1,400 commissioned field agents covering 13,000 Councils. Each agent is responsible for roughly a thousand members and their immediate families. It is the field agents who have sold and managed the $55 billion worth of life insurance policies currently in force across the United States. These aren't ordinary insurance salesmen. As a group, the field agents hold themselves to a very high standard, and the Knights continue to earn the coveted Insurance Marketplace Standards Association (IMSA) seal of approval for ethical marketing, sales, and practices.

Dan Sieve wasn't just a good field agent; he was among the best agents in the Order's history. As a field agent he wrote more than 2,000 applications and more than $72 million in life insurance. He never missed his sales quota. From 1997 to 2000, as a general agent in Missouri, his office wrote more than $91 million in new policies. Seven different times, he qualified for the Supreme Knight's Club—an award for the top 75 producers in the nation. He was a Chartered Life Underwriter, Chartered Financial Consultant, and Fraternal Insurance Counselor Fellow. His enthusiasm for protecting the families of the Knights entrusted to his care was unparalleled.

"There was no stopping Dan once he made the Knights of Columbus his life," said Donald Elbert, the Grand Knight of Sieve's Council. "Dan was one who sought to do the impossible."

Sieve did more than sell life insurance to protect members and their families; he also recruited men to join the Knights, believing that they could join no better organization. By mid-2001, at only 44 years old, he'd brought in 525 new members, the second highest total ever. Had he lived a longer life, one thing is reasonably certain: he would have come close to, if not broken, the all-time record held by Thomas Stelmar, Sr. (also a field agent) of Our Lady of the Lake Council 9337 in Rockwall, Texas.

But on May 1, 2001, as Dan was working at his desk at home, catching up on some paperwork, he quietly died.

Some people's lives reveal a perfect synergy between their faith and their work. Their jobs are an extension of who they are and what they believe and practice. This certainly describes Dan Sieve. Born on December 14, 1956, and raised in Washington, Missouri, Dan grew up in the eastern part of the state, and attended East Central College in Union. In 1978, he joined Seisl Council 1121 of the Knights of Columbus. Two years later he was elected Grand Knight and he also served as Faithful Navigator of his Fourth Degree Assembly. By 1981, he had been named Knight of the Year. In 1984 he became a field agent, one of the life insurance salesmen who protect the families of the Knights and form the financial foundation of the Order.

To say this came as a shock to everyone who knew him is an understatement. His passing was devastating to his wife, Donna, to his two young children, Timothy and Brian, to his coworkers, his clients, everyone at St. Gertrude's Church, his brothers in the Order, and his entire community. More than anyone else in Washington, Missouri, or the surrounding area, Dan personified the Knights of Columbus and its service to others. He had not only sold life insurance policies to families throughout the region but may people thought of him as a friend. He was a rock, one of those steady, dependable individuals whom you just assume will always be there when you need him. Suddenly he was gone and deeply missed; those he left behind now had to look for the resilience and strength inside themselves that they had drawn from Dan for so long.

At his memorial service, speakers drew comparisons between Dan and Father McGivney, the founder of the Knights, who also died very young, at age 38. Both men lived short lives but achieved more in the few years they were given than many others do in twice this amount of time. Both left behind a legacy of service to others that became an example for all who would become Knights. Dan raised the standard for anyone working as a field agent or recruiting new members. His impact was profound. More than 50 Knights from Fourth Degree assemblies around Missouri came and stood vigil at Dan's wake. His funeral was attended by dignitaries from across the Midwest, as well as the Order's Senior Vice-President of Agencies and Marketing, Thomas P. Smith, Jr.

Following the service, Timothy Mathews, a field agent at the time, spoke of how his former boss had taken care of him after his first wife had passed away in 1989. He'd never forgotten what this had meant to him. The town of Washington had lost more than a father, a husband, a friend, and an unparalleled businessman.

"Dan's life was the Knights of Columbus," Mathews said, "from the time he woke up in the morning until the time he went to sleep…He wasn't out for the glory but out for the membership and the individual member."

Dan Sieve didn't seek fame, nor did he want praise, but the way he lived his life inspired many. His devotion to the Knights and his desire to protect families is an example of service that deserves to be remembered.

Family photograph of Dan Sieve and his wife, Donna, and their two children.

David P. Hessling

The day the USS Cole was attacked by terrorists off the coast of Yemen, killing 17 American sailors, David (Dave) Hessling was working in Millington, Tennessee, as a computer specialist in the Casualty Operations Division of the Navy Personnel Command. His job typically involved managing databases and building web pages. But that day in October 2000 would be different. As he was sitting at his desk, the Division's toll-free number began to ring, and the calls just kept coming in. Relatives of Navy personnel had seen news coverage of the attack on television and wanted to know if their loved ones were all right. Hessling's job suddenly changed from a technician dealing with computers to a counselor dealing with human beings in crisis.

"My work now went above and beyond the realm of a computer specialist," he says. "I had to deal with a lot of powerful emotions. I fielded a number of phone calls from those who'd just lost a husband or brother or son, and I had no preparation for doing this."

Though he had not been trained by the Navy for this kind of challenge, David had gathered a lot of experience and strength during a decade of service to the Church and the Knights of Columbus, and it served him well on October 12, 2000.

"After the Cole bombing," he says, "I called my brother Knights for support and that always helped. I'd talked with them in the past about things, but now this contact became even more important."

Hessling also credits the Rosary, a devotion that all Knights are encouraged to pray, for providing him with spiritual strength during those stressful days. "If I lay in bed at night and couldn't fall asleep, I said the rosary and that brought me rest. I would say it until I found the peace of mind to go to sleep. When I really needed help the most to cope with my job, I felt like I was part of a big family, and I love big families."

For a month after the tragedy, Hessling helped families get to the hospital bedsides of those who'd been injured in the Cole bombing, and assisted those attending memorial services for victims who had died. His organizational skills, which he'd honed in the Knights of Columbus, were very useful now.

A past Grand Knight of Covington (Tennessee) Council 10641, Hessling had overseen the Council's activities at the Memphis Motorsports Park and those at the Liberty Bowl, where he and his fellow Knights raised money for charity at concession stands. A resident of Atoka, he volunteered at the fire department and helped write its grant proposal, which won the department a $110,000 award from the Federal Emergency Management Agency. With the Knights, he'd volunteered for the Special Olympics and been in charge of maintaining and updating the Tennessee State Council website. He also was a strong supporter of Associated Catholic Charities. All these experiences, and the emotional support of his brother Knights, came into play that fall.

The "big family" he'd been part of in the Order now supported him when he needed it most, and he performed so well in the aftermath of the Cole bombing that he was honored in January 2001 with the American Legion Distinguished Service Award.

All this prepared Hessling for being called up in 2003 by the Army Reserve and put on active duty for two years in Alexandria, Virginia. He chose to work in Army Human Resources, and currently has the job of notifying families whose relatives have suffered injuries in combat in Iraq or Afghanistan. It's another huge and emotionally demanding task: in 2003–2004, he phoned 4,000 families with this news. Every call was difficult, some more than others. Eighty-five per cent of the injuries were minor but hundreds involved losing an arm or leg, or suffering permanent brain damage. When a soldier is killed, families are notified in person, but when they are injured, the contact is made over the phone. Those calls were made by Dave Hessling.

"This is much more stressful than computer work," he says. "This is all about human beings."

He credits his spiritual background and especially his work as a Knight with allowing him to serve his country well during a time of war.

"The Order stands for helping people who really need help," he says. "That's what our Council does and that's what I've been doing since I went on active duty, but the Order also helps me."

"When I'm on leave, I go home and spend time with the Knights. I just like being around them, talking with them. They give me balance, stability, and comfort when I need these things the most. They keep me connected to the Church and to who I am. They give to me so that I can give to others."

The USS Cole after it was attacked off the coast of Yemen on October 12, 2000.

Robert D. Wolf, Jr.

In just a few short years, Robert Wolf has served as a Grand Knight in Scottsbluff, Nebraska, and was honored as the 2003 Nebraska "Knight of the Year." But he wouldn't have even become a Knight if not for his youngest son, James. In 2000, Robert and his son were invited to a

pancake breakfast at the local Council Hall, where they enjoyed themselves immensely. Jamie liked it so much that he was considering signing up for the Knights that very morning, but Bob wasn't so sure. He took his son aside and made a deal: he'd take the plunge, but only if Jamie went first. Before the breakfast was finished, James, who had just graduated from high school, had signed up to become the youngest member of the Council. Five minutes later, his dad kept his word and joined too. James's grandfather, Robert Sr., was also a member, and so the Wolfs now had three generations of Knights. Robert Jr., who runs a tire store in Scottsbluff, doesn't do things halfway. Not only did he become a Knight, he soon became Grand Knight of Father Timothy P. Molony Council 2681.

For the past quarter century, the Council has run a Christmastime "Toys for Tots" program, and it's a yearlong undertaking. Every January, they start collecting toys, books, and clothes for disadvantaged kids in the North Platte River Valley in western Nebraska. As the weather warms up, a local bank puts a 40-foot semi-trailer out on the street, and people come by and fill it with donations. The local Harley-Davidson club makes a toy run for the Knights, and in return is served a huge lunch at the Council hall. As the holiday season approaches, the Knights work closely with Panhandle Community Services to find the people most in need in the area. The Council makes a special point of helping those on welfare and migrant families. They keep a special eye out for situations where the father is in jail and can't provide for his children at Christmas.

"The Knights were founded by Father McGivney to take care of widows and orphans," Robert says, "and that's what we're meant to do. We're just carrying on that tradition."

All the gifts are taken to the Scottsbluff high school gym where they're sorted, placed in large bags, and prepared for distribution. A few days before Christmas, Knights fan out across the Valley and deliver the toys door-to-door, along with a food basket. The program now reaches nearly a thousand youngsters.

"People around here talk about how much the Knights do for them," Robert says, "but we get more out of this than the children do. These are the only presents that some of these kids get all year long. When you deliver toys to five or six kids in a home and they don't have anything there for Christmas—or even a Christmas tree—you see them beam at you and you know you've made a difference. That expression on their face is why you became a Knight."

During the 2003 holiday season, the Scottsbluff council learned that the Samaritan House in Denver had lost its funding and couldn't afford to give presents to children in the Mile High City. Wolf contacted a priest in Denver and made arrangements to load a semi with extra gifts that his local Knights had collected; they shipped 19 pallets filled with gifts to Denver, and the big load made it there just in time. It was Christmas as usual at the Samaritan House and children all over the city were thrilled.

Bob Wolf had also been blessed with a very supportive wife; Chris encouraged his work with the Knights and she was very active in the Foster Grandparents program at Panhandle Community Services. While Robert was running the Council in Scottsbluff, their youngest son had taken on another job. After high school, James joined the army and prepared to go to war in Iraq with the 52nd Engineer Battalion. In 2003, the Knights of Columbus gave James, along with tens of thousands of other American soldiers fighting abroad, Armed With the Faith, a spiritual handbook recently published by the Order. He kept it with his other valued possessions until the very end. On November 6, 2003, the 21-year-old Nebraskan was killed near Mosul, Iraq, after an improvised explosive device exploded near his convoy. When his family received his effects back from the government, they saw a military ID card, a Blockbuster card, a pocket rosary, and his Third Degree Knights of Columbus card. The Wolf family immediately began receiving letters from Councils all over the state, expressing support for them and prayers for James. Hundreds from around Nebraska came to his memorial service and a Knights of Columbus honor guard was there to escort his casket. Bob and Chris

also began spending time with other parents who had lost a child, offering them support and comfort. Their faith sustained them during these difficult times.

In the spring of 2004, Jamie's fellow Knights held a tribute for the fallen soldier at the local hall, where they talked about his infectious grin, his commitment to others, and how much he'd loved the Order. Everyone remembered seeing James enjoying himself at the hall, but nobody was more grateful for these memories than his father. If it hadn't been for his son, Robert Wolf would never have known the feeling that comes with helping kids in need. He'd never have seen the smiles on the faces of those children as the toys were being delivered right before Christmas, nor really understood what it means to be a Knight.

James Wolf's dog tag and cross, which were presented to his family after his death.

Personal effects of James Wolf.

Ted van der Zalm

When Ted van der Zalm was a boy in St. Catharines, Ontario, Canada, he learned many things from his father, but one lesson stood out above all: it is better to give than to receive. In Ted's case, the giving has never been confined to conventional gifts. As a youngster, Ted had known that his father was active in the Knights of Columbus and made part of his mission traveling abroad to help people in developing nations. When Ted came of age, he too joined St. Catharines Council 1394. He helped with fund-raising efforts, sold tickets, and got sponsors for the local turkey raffle. But as much as he loved his work helping the poor, it often took him far to another part of the world. And wherever Ted went, he took along his boundless enthusiasm and the four words he was most identified with at the St. Vincent de Paul Parish in Niagara-on-the-Lake, Ontario: "Isn't our God awesome?" Many people who watched Ted serve the poor were filled with awe as well.

In 1985, he first went to Tanzania in East Africa as a volunteer missionary. There he received a very humbling lesson regarding all the things he'd taken for granted living in Canada, such as being able to draw and drink a glass of pure water—a true luxury in his new home. His job in Tanzania was to build windmills and drill wells in impoverished rural villages and to find a clean, reliable water source for the local population. Before he and other missionaries arrived, the poor walked five miles each morning looking for a bucket of clean water. Many couldn't find clean water so they returned to their mud huts with only a brown, bacteria-infested liquid that stunted growth and spread diseases such as malaria.

The water wasn't the only dangerous thing in Tanzania. Once, after Ted's vehicle broke, he was hitchhiking, and he got picked up by some men. The driver crashed the car into a group of Tanzanian soldiers, killing one of them. The driver and the other passengers fled, leaving Ted alone with the surviving soldiers, who beat Ted into a coma. When he came out of it, he forgave his assailants as a Christian and a Knight committed to charity.

After three years in Tanzania, Ted met Miriam. The two of them were married and worked side by side for seven years in East Africa. During that time Ted earned a pilot's license. In Tanzania, he flew a plane to transport doctors and patients from rural areas to modern medical facilities. One day the engine failed and Ted was forced to land the damaged craft in a sugar field. This made him more certain than ever that God was keeping him alive for a reason; obviously, there were still missions for him to fulfill.

The couple's first child, Sarah, was born in Tanzania and a short while later, they moved back to Ontario to raise their family. Ted became a religion teacher at Denis Morris High School in St. Catharines, but he badly missed working in the Third World. When he and Miriam learned of a chance to go to help the people of Guatemala, they packed up their belongings and their five children and headed south. The United Nations had recently published a report stating that "a person dies every eight seconds due to water-related diseases," and the van der Zalms were committed to changing this tragic reality. For six months they lived in tents, building an irrigation system that would bring clean water to villagers. Ted made enormous personal sacrifices in his work for others. Once, while digging a 75-foot deep well, he became so exhausted and dehydrated that he lost vision in one eye. Despite these hardships, he brought 30 new wells to the local population. Every day they spent in Guatemala, the van der Zalms saw how much they had to be grateful for.

Back in Ontario, Ted started a project at Denis Morris High School in which every new student was given a personal Catholic Youth Bible. Students used the Bibles for educational purposes, and upon graduation they took the Bibles with them to help in their journey through adulthood. For Ted, the project was comparable to what he'd done in Tanzania and Guatemala. He'd set in motion things that would benefit others for decades to come.

In the fall of 2004, another opportunity arose for the family to go back to Guatemala, but this time they had to provide their own financial backing. They mortgaged their home to buy a well-digging rig, and off they went with their kids in tow. They drove the digging equipment and support vehicles from Ontario to Guatemala. The work in Guatemala not only sprang from the values and ethics of the Order, but now, the Knights themselves were directly involved in aiding his efforts. State Deputies in all of the regions the van der Zalms passed through on their way south provided the family with meals, a place to spend the night, and gas money for the next leg of their journey.

When Ted and Miriam's children traveled with their parents they learned the value of giving help to people living in such dire poverty. The children saw what it means to be charitable and humble—and to make genuine sacrifices for others. Ted also started an organization called Wells of Hope, which raises funds for future irrigation projects in rural Guatemala. In 2004, the van der Zalms won the Ontario State Council's "Family of the Year," and finished as runners up for the International Family of the year award.

As Father Paul J. McDonald wrote in his endorsement, "Their extraordinary devotion to the poor is inspiring. May their enthusiasm spread to more and more."

Guatemalan women filling water pitchers at a well built by the Wells of Hope organization.

Normand Letourneau

In the 1890s, Father John Kavanagh moved to Montreal from New York State with the desire to establish the Knights of Columbus north of the border. A member of Plattsburgh Council 255 in Cliff Haven, New York, the Irish-American priest was determined to put down the Order's roots among the French Canadians in Quebec. On November 25, 1897, his vision was realized, and Dr. James J. Guerin, the former mayor of Montreal, become the first Grand Knight on Canadian soil. With Montreal Council 284 in place in Quebec, the Order would spread out across Canada in all directions, much as it had done in the western United States, and as it would soon do in Mexico and the Philippines. The Order was becoming a truly international organization.

When Father Kavanagh brought the Order northward, he wanted to share its fellowship with future generations of Catholic men like Normand Letourneau of Legal, Alberta. In 1949, Letourneau joined the Knights and in the years to come, he would hold every office in Legal Council 3223. Normand was active in the Knights from the moment of his initiation. He recruited his father into the Order, his four brothers, three of his sons, two of his grandchildren, many others outside his family, and he's still working on signing up two more grandkids. Four generations of Letourneau men are now part of Council 3223.

Normand's bustling clan is legendary around Legal, where they make up a significant portion of the town's population of 1,095. They are such an integral part of the town that when the local historical society wanted a book to be written in celebration of Legal's centennial, Normand and his wife, Fernande, were instrumental in making the book a reality. And the Knights of Columbus have also been active in preserving the history of Legal. In one important project, they sponsored the painting of a mural of Bishop Emile Legal, after whom the town is named. The 8-by-20-foot mural was unveiled in 2002 at St. Emile's Church.

Since the middle of the last century, Normand and Fernande, his wife of more than five decades, have been the lifeblood of the local church, Council 3223, and their hometown in Alberta. Normand and his sons have taken part in parish bingo games, parish parades, and retreats. They've served on the hospital board, participated in hockey, baseball, and soccer games, and headed fund-raising drives. In 1952, the Knights purchased new church bells for the parish.

In 1986, Normand's oldest son, Robert, ran a Knights' project to design a community park and in 1992 Normand's third son, Denis, oversaw the construction of a specially designed new home for a brother Knight, Gerald St.Martin, who was afflicted with multiple sclerosis. The Knights also have worked to keep Alberta's highways clean, and helped their neighbors rebuild after a barn or store burned to the ground. In short, if there was a good deed to be done in the area, it was the Knights, many of them Letourneaus, who most often answered the call. In 1993, in the tradition of his father, Normand's fourth son, Gerald, offered his services at the local John Paul II Bible School and fixed the plumbing and heating for free.

If a volunteer was needed for any reason, the Letourneaus were the first ones called because everyone knew the answer would be "yes." As Normand's fellow Knights put it when recommending the Letourneaus as "Family of the Year" in Alberta in 2004: "If it wasn't for Normand and his boys, the Legal Council would have folded a long time ago. Some of them have moved away and others are working out of town. Their absence is greatly felt throughout the Church and the community."

In 1984, when Pope John Paul II visited Alberta, Normand was part of the Fourth Degree Honor Guard at the Mass site in Namao. In March 2002, Normand's granddaughter, a talented singer named Janelle, flew to Paris to promote World Youth Day at the Conference of Bishops. From Paris she went to Rome and sang in St. Peter's Square, where she met Pope John Paul II. She has continued to travel all over the world, providing a music ministry for young people, winning several important music industry awards, and recording two popular CDs of Christian music.

In his eighties now, Normand remains heavily involved with the Knights and makes sure that his sons show up at the Order's functions. It has been that way since 1949.

"At community events," one recent tribute to the Letourneaus read, "you can see the whole family there, whether it be just to attend, or helping out with several volunteer groups. You can easily tell this family is very close and always ready and willing to lend a helping hand wherever it is needed. God is very present and active in this family, blessing them with fond memories and great amounts of love and joy. These are just some of the commitments this family has made toward the Church, the community, and the Knights of Columbus."

The Letourneaus would certainly have made Father Kavanagh and Dr. Guerin very proud.

The Letourneau family have passed the Knights of Columbus tradition down through several generations.

Credits

DeSilver, Charles, *The First Landing of Columbus in the New World.* Courtesy of the Knights of Columbus Museum, Matthew S. and Hedy M. Santangelo Collection.

Father Michael J. McGivney. Courtesy of the Knights of Columbus Museum.

Fighting 69th at Mass. Library of Congress, Prints & Photographs Division, Civil War Photographs, reproduction number, LC-DIG-CWPB-06586.

Charter of the Knights of Columbus. Courtesy of the Knights of Columbus Supreme Council Archives.

Columbus Day Parade in Washington, D.C. Courtesy of the Knights of Columbus Supreme Council Photo Archives.

James T. Mullen. Courtesy of the Knights of Columbus Supreme Council Photo Archives.

St. Mary's Church in 1885. Courtesy of the Knights of Columbus Supreme Council Photo Archives.

Endowment upon the death of James T. Mullen, 1891. Courtesy of the Knights of Columbus Supreme Council Archives.

James B. Connolly. Courtesy of Colby College Special Collections, Waterville, Maine.

Columbia, July 1932. Courtesy of Knights of Columbus Supreme Council Archives.

William C. Prout. Courtesy of the Massachusetts State Council of the Knights of Columbus.

Program for the William C. Prout Memorial Games. Courtesy of the Knights of Columbus Supreme Council Archives.

Edward F. McSweeney by Angelo. © 2005 The Philip Lief Group, Inc.

Three monographs published by the Historical Commission. Courtesy of the Knights of Columbus Supreme Council Archives.

John H. Reddin, Supreme Master of the Fourth Degree. Courtesy of the Knights

of Columbus Supreme Council Photo Archives.

Supreme Officers and Directors of the Knights of Columbus, Chicago, December 17, 1932. Courtesy of the Knights of Columbus Supreme Council Photo Archives.

Patrick H. Joyce. Courtesy of the Chicago Historical Society.

Chicago Great Western Locomotive. Courtesy of the Collection of the Chicago & North Western Historical Society.

Connie Mack. © National Baseball Hall of Fame Library, Cooperstown, New York.

Clay bust of Connie Mack. © 2005 Patrick Korten.

Father William Davitt. Courtesy of the Knights of Columbus Supreme Council Photo Archives.

K. of C. Hut, France, circa 1917. Courtesy of the Knights of Columbus Supreme Council Photo Archives.

Daniel Joseph Daly. Courtesy of the National Archives, reproduction number, 127-N-515597.

USS Daly. © The United States Naval Institute.

Joyce Kilmer by Underwood & Underwood, 1917. Digital restoration © Miriam A. Kilmer.

Papers carried by Joyce Kilmer. Courtesy of Miriam A. Kilmer.

Dr. Claude Brown. Courtesy of the Knights of Columbus Supreme Council Photo Archives.

Memorial Service of Dr. Brown. Courtesy of Lieutenant Colonel Claude Brown memorial album, The University of Western Ontario Archives.

Father John Devalles. Courtesy of the National Archives, reproduction number 111-SC-11355.

Letter written by Father Devalles, September 23, 1917. Courtesy of the Knights of Columbus Supreme Council Archives.

George Herman "Babe" Ruth. © National Baseball Hall of Fame Library, Cooperstown, New York.

Babe Ruth at Knickerbocker Hospital, April 15, 1930. Courtesy of the Knights of Columbus Supreme Council Photo Archives.

Father Luis Batis Sainz. Courtesy of the Knights of Columbus Supreme Council Photo Archives.

Father José María Robles Hurtado. Courtesy of the Knights of Columbus Supreme Council Photo Archives.

Father Mateo Correa Magallanes. Courtesy of the Knights of Columbus Supreme Council Photo Archives.

Father Rodrigo Aguilar Aleman by Angelo. © 2005 The Philip Lief Group, Inc.

Father Miguel de la Mora. Courtesy of the Knights of Columbus Supreme Council Photo Archives.

Father Pedro de Jesús Maldonado Lucero. Courtesy of the Knights of Columbus Supreme Council Photo Archives.

Father Michael J. Ahern, S.J. Courtesy of Canisius College Archives, Buffalo, New York.

Ahern, Levi, and Ratcliffe, 1938. Courtesy of the Knights of Columbus Supreme Council Photo Archives.

Al Smith. Courtesy of the Knights of Columbus Supreme Council Photo Archives.

Al Smith on the campaign trail, circa 1928. © Corbis.

Reagan family Christmas card, circa 1916–1917. Courtesy of the Ronald Reagan Library.

President Ronald Reagan speaking, 1982. Courtesy of the Knights of Columbus Supreme Council Photo Archives.

Isaias Edralin by Vince Natale. © 2005 The Philip Lief Group, Inc.

Filipino survivors, February 23, 1945. © The Art Archive / National Archives Washington DC.

George Willmann. Copyright and courtesy of the Knights of Columbus Philippines.

George Willmann at a Knights of Columbus event. Copyright and courtesy of the Knights of Columbus Philippines.

Myles Connolly. Courtesy of the Academy of Motion Picture Arts and Sciences.

Mr. Smith Goes to Washington, 1939. © Columbia / The Kobal Collection.

Oscar Ledesma. Copyright and courtesy of the Knights of Columbus Philippines.

Oscar Ledesma and George Willmann. Copyright and courtesy of the Knights of Columbus Philippines.

Ernest King. Courtesy of the Knights of Columbus Supreme Council Photo Archives.

Ernest King at the Supreme Council meeting, 1976. Courtesy of the Knights of Columbus Supreme Council Photo Archives.

Father William Ryan, *The Oblate World*. Courtesy of Deacon Kenneth N. Ryan. © Oblate Communications.

Father William Ryan. Courtesy of Deacon Kenneth N. Ryan.

Jorge Hyatt by Angelo. © 2005 The Philip Lief Group, Inc.

Gifts from Havana. Courtesy of the Knights of Columbus Supreme Council Photo Archives.

John F. Kennedy, circa 1960–1964. Courtesy of Cecil Stoughton, White House/John Fitzgerald Kennedy Library, Boston.

John Fitzgerald Kennedy and Jacqueline Lee Bouvier. St. Mary's Church, Newport, Rhode Island, September 12, 1953. Courtesy of the John Fitzgerald Kennedy Library, Boston.

Exemplification of the Forth Degree, Fall River, Massachusetts, May 30, 1954. Courtesy of the Knights of Columbus Supreme Council Photo Archives.

Index of Names

James T. Mullen ❖ James B. Connolly ❖ William C. Prout ❖ Edward F. McSweeney ❖ John H. Red
Joyce Kilmer ❖ Dr. Claude Brown ❖ Father John B. DeValles ❖ George Herman "Babe" Ruth
Father Miguel de la Mora ❖ Father Rodrigo Aguilar Alemán ❖ Father Pedro de Jesús Maldonado L
Father George Willmann ❖ Myles E. Connolly ❖ Oscar Ledesma ❖ Ernest I. King ❖ Father William P.
Carlos M. Rodríguez ❖ John W. McCormack ❖ Father Charles J. Watters ❖ Joseph A. Sullivan ❖ J
Matthew C. Gannon ❖ Chris Godfrey ❖ Paul D. Scully-Power ❖ Robert Sargent Shriver ❖ Virgil C. D
Judge William F. Downes ❖ Donald D. Lederhos ❖ Raymond L. Flynn ❖ Father Ronald P. Pytel
Kevin Lopresti ❖ Daniel D. Sieve ❖ David P. Hessling ❖ Robert D. Wolf ❖ Ted van der Zalm ❖ Nor
John H. Reddin ❖ Patrick H. Joyce ❖ Connie Mack ❖ Father William F. Davitt ❖ Sergeant Major Danie
Father Luis Batis Sainz ❖ Father José María Robles Hurtado ❖ Father Mateo Correa Megallanes ❖
Father Michael J. Ahern ❖ Alfred E. Smith ❖ John Edward Reagan ❖ Father Isaias X. Edralin ❖ Fat
Jorge J. Hyatt ❖ John Fitzgerald Kennedy ❖ Vincent T. Lombardi ❖ Major General Patrick H. Brady ❖ Carl
Harry E. McKillop ❖ Ronald A. Guidry ❖ Hilario G. Davide ❖ Alfred F. "Bud" Jetty ❖ Matthew
Father Thomas A. Mulcrone ❖ Paul E. Nollette ❖ Beryl D. Jones ❖ Steve Lopez ❖ John Whyta
Lieutenant Daniel O'Callaghan ❖ Captain Alfredo N. Fuentes ❖ Vincent P. Valerio ❖ Paul Marretti ❖ Kevi

James T. Mullen ❖ James B. Connolly ❖ William C. Prout ❖ Edward F. McSweeney ❖ John H. Red
Joyce Kilmer ❖ Dr. Claude Brown ❖ Father John B. DeValles ❖ George Herman "Babe" Ruth
Father Miguel de la Mora ❖ Father Rodrigo Aguilar Alemán ❖ Father Pedro de Jesús Maldonado L
Father George Willmann ❖ Myles E. Connolly ❖ Oscar Ledesma ❖ Ernest I. King ❖ Father William P.
Carlos M. Rodríguez ❖ John W. McCormack ❖ Father Charles J. Watters ❖ Joseph A. Sullivan ❖ Jo
Matthew C. Gannon ❖ Chris Godfrey ❖ Paul D. Scully-Power ❖ Robert Sargent Shriver ❖ Virgil C. D
Judge William F. Downes ❖ Donald D. Lederhos ❖ Raymond L. Flynn ❖ Father Ronald P. Pytel
Kevin Lopresti ❖ Daniel D. Sieve ❖ David P. Hessling ❖ Robert D. Wolf ❖ Ted van der Zalm ❖ Nor
John H. Reddin ❖ Patrick H. Joyce ❖ Connie Mack ❖ Father William F. Davitt ❖ Sergeant Major Danie
Father Luis Batis Sainz ❖ Father José María Robles Hurtado ❖ Father Mateo Correa Megallanes ❖
Father Michael J. Ahern ❖ Alfred E. Smith ❖ John Edward Reagan ❖ Father Isaias X. Edralin ❖ Fat
Jorge J. Hyatt ❖ John Fitzgerald Kennedy ❖ Vincent T. Lombardi ❖ Major General Patrick H. Brady ❖ Carl
Harry E. McKillop ❖ Ronald A. Guidry ❖ Hilario G. Davide ❖ Alfred F. "Bud" Jetty ❖ Matthew
Father Thomas A. Mulcrone ❖ Paul E. Nollette ❖ Beryl D. Jones ❖ Steve Lopez ❖ John Whyta
Lieutenant Daniel O'Callaghan ❖ Captain Alfredo N. Fuentes ❖ Vincent P. Valerio ❖ Paul Marretti ❖ Kevi